FRANCHISE YOUR AYURVEDA CLINIC

(STEP BY STEP GUIDE TO SCALE YOUR BRAND)

DR MUKESH AGGARWAL

Made with ❤ on the Notion Press Platform
www.notionpress.com

Preface

Welcome to "Franchise Your Ayurveda Clinic: A Step-By-Step Guide to Scale Your Brand." This book is a culmination of my years of experience and expertise in the field of Ayurveda, coupled with a deep passion for entrepreneurship and franchising. It is aimed at Ayurveda practitioners, business enthusiasts, and anyone interested in expanding the reach of this ancient healing system.

The world of Ayurveda is rich, diverse, and has an extraordinary potential to transform lives. With its holistic approach to well-being, Ayurveda offers a unique and time-tested path to health and wellness. This book is not only about harnessing the power of Ayurveda but also about sharing it with the world.

In the pages that follow, you'll embark on a journey to understand the essence of Ayurveda, explore the opportunities it offers for franchising, and learn the step-by-step process to establish and expand your Ayurveda clinic. We'll delve into the philosophy and principles of Ayurveda, the various treatments and therapies it encompasses, and the fundamentals of franchising. You'll gain insights into setting up your clinic, addressing legal and financial considerations, marketing and branding, and ensuring the quality and success of your franchise.

Throughout the book, you'll find case studies highlighting successful Ayurveda clinic franchises, offering real-world examples of how this ancient science can thrive in a modern, entrepreneurial context.

I hope this book becomes your trusted guide on your journey to franchising an Ayurveda clinic, sharing the wisdom of Ayurveda with a wider audience, and contributing to the well-being of countless individuals.

Your commitment to this path is commendable, and I am excited to share this knowledge with you. Let's begin this enlightening and transformative journey together.

-Dr Mukesh Aggarwal

Acknowledgements

I would like to express my deepest gratitude to the many individuals who have played an instrumental role in the creation of this book. Without their support, dedication, and expertise, this project would not have come to fruition.

First and foremost, I extend my heartfelt appreciation to the practitioners, scholars, and experts in the field of Ayurveda whose knowledge and wisdom have enriched the content of this book. Your commitment to the ancient principles of Ayurveda and your willingness to share your insights have been invaluable.

I also wish to acknowledge the franchisees and entrepreneurs who have ventured into the world of Ayurveda clinics, embracing this opportunity and contributing to the growth of our brand. Your experiences and success stories serve as inspiration for others.

I am grateful to my team, who worked tirelessly on every aspect of this book, from research and content development to editing and design. Your dedication to excellence is truly commendable.

My appreciation goes out to my family and friends, whose unwavering support and encouragement kept me motivated throughout this journey.

Finally, I extend my thanks to the readers and aspiring entrepreneurs who have chosen to explore the world of Ayurveda franchising. I hope this book serves as a valuable guide on your path to success.

Thank you all for being a part of this endeavor and for your collective efforts in bringing the vision of Ayurveda clinic franchising to life.

-Dr. Mukesh Aggarwal

CONTENT

Section 1

AYURVEDA AND FRANCHISING FUN-DAMENTALS

CHAPTER ONE

INTRODUCTION

HIGHLIGHTS

The chapter introduces Ayurveda as the "Science of Life," exploring its holistic principles, and then outlines a compelling opportunity in Ayurveda clinic franchises, detailing their global appeal, franchise model advantages, and alignment with wellness trends, concluding with the purpose and scope of a comprehensive guide for individuals interested in franchising their Ayurveda clinics.

ESSENCE OF AYURVEDA

Ayurveda, a system of traditional medicine that has its roots in ancient India, is often referred to as the "Science of Life." Its essence lies in a holistic approach to health and wellness, emphasizing the balance of mind, body, and spirit. This age-old practice is not merely a system of curing ailments but a way of life that promotes harmony and well-being.

At the heart of Ayurveda is the belief that each individual is unique, and their health is influenced by a combination of physical, mental, and emotional factors. These factors are categorized into three doshas: Vata, Pitta, and Kapha. The balance of these doshas is key to maintaining good health, while their imbalance can lead to diseases.

Ayurveda offers a comprehensive approach to diagnosis and treatment. Practitioners consider a person's constitution, known as "Prakriti," and their current state of health, known as "Vikriti." By understanding these aspects, Ayurvedic healers prescribe personalized remedies that can include diet, lifestyle adjustments, herbal medicines, and therapeutic practices.

The essence of Ayurveda is not limited to the treatment of diseases but extends to the prevention of illnesses and the promotion of longevity. It emphasizes the importance of a balanced and wholesome diet, regular exercise, and proper stress management. Furthermore, it recognizes the profound connection between the mind and body, highlighting the impact of emotional and mental well-being on one's physical health.

Fig: 1.1 Decoction made from medicinal herbs

In addition to its holistic approach, Ayurveda places a strong emphasis on natural remedies. The use of herbs, minerals, and other natural substances is integral to Ayurvedic treatment. These remedies are believed to work in harmony with the body, minimizing side effects and promoting long-term healing.

Ayurveda's essence also includes the recognition of the interplay between an individual and their environment. It takes into account the seasons, climate, and geographic location, as these factors can influence health. This wisdom is evident in Ayurvedic recommendations on seasonal diets and lifestyle adjustments.

While Ayurveda has a rich history dating back thousands of years, its essence remains relevant in the modern world. As people seek holistic and natural approaches to health, Ayurveda's principles continue to offer valuable insights and practices. It complements conventional medicine, focusing on prevention and wellness, making it an increasingly popular choice for those seeking a balanced and harmonious life.

In conclusion, Ayurveda encapsulates the essence of holistic healing, emphasizing the individual's unique constitution, the balance of doshas, natural remedies, and the intricate connection between mind, body, and spirit. Its timeless wisdom provides a roadmap to wellness, and as the world becomes more health-conscious, the relevance of Ayurveda in promoting holistic well-being is more significant than ever. Ayurveda is not just a system of medicine; it's a profound philosophy that guides individuals toward a life of balance and vitality.

THE OPPORTUNITY IN AYURVEDA CLINIC FRANCHISE

Ayurveda, the ancient system of holistic medicine that originated in India, has gained immense popularity globally for its natural and holistic approach to health and wellness. As the demand for alternative and complementary healthcare options continues to grow, there is a significant opportunity in Ayurveda clinic franchises. These franchises offer a unique blend of traditional healing practices and modern business models, creating a promising venture for both entrepreneurs and health enthusiasts.

Rising Interest in Holistic Health: One of the primary factors driving the opportunity in Ayurveda clinic franchises is the increasing awareness and interest in holistic health. People are seeking alternatives to conventional medicine and are drawn to Ayurveda's focus on balance, natural remedies, and individualized treatments. This demand presents a thriving market for Ayurveda clinics.

Cultural Exchange and Globalization: The globalization of cultures and practices has made Ayurveda more accessible worldwide. Ayurveda's core principles are adaptable to various cultures and can be integrated with local healthcare systems. This adaptability makes it easier to establish Ayurveda clinic franchises in different regions, attracting a diverse clientele.

Franchise Model: The franchise model is a practical and efficient way to expand Ayurveda clinics. Entrepreneurs can leverage the established brand, treatment protocols, and business support offered by the franchisor. This lowers the entry barriers and provides a ready-made framework for success.

Diverse Services: Ayurveda clinics can offer a range of services beyond traditional treatments, including wellness programs, yoga, meditation, and beauty therapies. This diversification appeals to a broader customer base, making Ayurveda clinics more attractive and profitable.

Wellness Tourism: Many regions around the world are capitalizing on wellness tourism. Ayurveda clinic franchises can tap into this growing trend by providing authentic Ayurvedic experiences to international visitors. These clinics often become sought-after destinations for wellness travelers.

Natural and Organic Trends: As the world increasingly embraces natural and organic products and practices, Ayurveda aligns well with these trends. The use of herbal medicines, organic ingredients, and eco-friendly practices in Ayurveda clinics resonates with environmentally conscious consumers.

Educational Opportunities: Ayurveda clinic franchises can also serve as centers for educating people about Ayurveda. Offering workshops, seminars, and training programs can generate additional revenue and establish the franchise as a trusted source of Ayurvedic knowledge.

Regulatory Support: In some countries, regulatory bodies are recognizing and regulating Ayurveda, which adds credibility to the industry. These regulations can benefit Ayurveda clinic franchises by ensuring quality and safety standards.

Community Impact: Ayurveda clinics often contribute positively to their communities by creating jobs, promoting local herbal cultivation, and raising awareness about healthy living. This community engagement can enhance the reputation and success of the franchise.

Long-Term Health Focus: Ayurveda promotes long-term health and prevention. This characteristic distinguishes it from many short-term healthcare solutions, making it appealing to individuals looking for sustainable well-being.

Conclusion, Ayurveda clinic franchises offer a unique opportunity to enter the expanding wellness and healthcare industry. Their holistic approach, adaptability, and alignment with global health trends make them an attractive prospect for both entrepreneurs and those passionate about holistic well-being. As Ayurveda continues to weave its way into the fabric of modern healthcare, the growth potential for Ayurveda clinic franchises is substantial, offering a harmonious blend of tradition and business innovation.

PURPOSE AND SCOPE OF ABOVE BOOK

Provide a comprehensive guide for individuals interested in franchising their Ayurveda clinics. The book aims to:

Educate Readers: It introduces readers to the essence of Ayurveda, highlighting the opportunity for franchising within this field.

Provide In-Depth Knowledge: It delves into the principles and practices of Ayurveda, including various treatments and therapies.

Explain Franchising: The book covers the fundamentals of franchising, detailing its categories, advantages, disadvantages, and the legal and regulatory aspects, especially in the context of India.

Guide on Preparation: It guides readers on how to prepare for their Ayurveda clinic franchise, from identifying their specialties and unique selling points to crafting a business concept and defining mission, vision, and core values.

Assist in Clinic Setup: It helps in selecting the right location, designing the clinic, and sourcing necessary medicines and equipment.

Address Legal and Financial Aspects: The book explains franchise agreements, financial planning, funding options, and the various costs associated with franchising.

Focus on Marketing and Branding: It offers insights into building an Ayurveda brand, implementing marketing strategies for franchise clinics, and both online and offline promotion.

` It covers the essential aspects of running a franchise, including creating operation manuals, appointing staff, training, scheduling patients, inventory management, and maintaining patient records.

Emphasize Quality Assurance: The book discusses the importance of maintaining high-quality standards and gathering patient feedback.

Encourage Growth: It guides on expanding the clinic network and innovating new services and products.

Look at Future Trends: The book touches upon future trends in franchising, ensuring that readers are aware of the evolving landscape.

Showcase Success Stories: It provides case studies of successful Ayurveda clinic franchises, offering real-world examples and inspiration.

Additionally, the book includes valuable resources and references such as Ayurveda texts, industry associations, and relevant websites to assist readers in their journey to franchise an Ayurveda clinic. The primary aim is to equip individuals with the knowledge and guidance needed to successfully expand their Ayurveda clinic through franchising.

CHAPTER TWO

UNDERSTANDING AYURVEDA

HIGHLIGHTS

Exploring Ayurveda's ancient wisdom, this chapter delves into foundational principles like doshas and elemental concepts, showcasing its holistic approach through practices such as Panchakarma, Abhyanga, and Marma Therapy, emphasizing a unique blend of dietary guidelines, herbal medicine, and mind-body connection for individualized well-being in contemporary healthcare.

AYURVEDA PRINCIPLES AND PRACTICE

Ayurveda, often referred to as the "science of life," is an ancient system of medicine that has been practiced for thousands of years in India. Its principles and practices are deeply rooted in the philosophy of balance and harmony, focusing on the holistic well-being of an individual. This essay delves into the core principles and practices of Ayurveda, shedding light on its unique approach to health and wellness.

FOUNDATIONAL PRINCIPLES OF AYURVEDA

Doshas: Ayurveda classifies individuals into three primary doshas: Vata, Pitta, and Kapha. These doshas represent the fundamental energies or constitutional types in the body. Understanding one's dosha is essential for tailoring health and lifestyle practices.

Prakriti and Vikriti: Ayurveda distinguishes between one's natural constitution (Prakriti) and their current state of health (Vikriti). A person's Prakriti is determined at birth, while Vikriti reflects their imbalances or ailments.

Panchamahabhutas: Ayurveda is rooted in the concept of the five fundamental elements - earth, water, fire, air, and ether. These elements combine to form the doshas and influence the body's physiological functions.

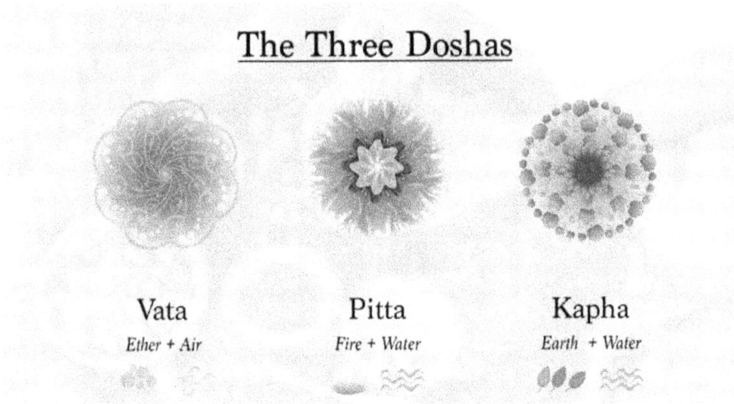

Fig: 2.1 Depiction of creation of tridoshas from panchmahabhutas

PRACTICES IN AYURVEDA

Dietary Guidelines: Ayurveda emphasizes the importance of a balanced and individualized diet. Foods are categorized based on their impact on the doshas, and individuals are advised to eat according to their constitution.

Herbal Medicine: Ayurveda employs a vast array of medicinal plants and herbs. Herbal remedies are used to restore balance and treat various ailments. These formulations are customized based on an individual's dosha.

Yoga and Meditation: Yoga and meditation are integral components of Ayurvedic practice. They promote physical and mental harmony, aiding in the prevention of diseases and the maintenance of overall health.

Panchakarma: Panchakarma is a detoxification process that involves various therapies like massage, herbal steam, and enemas. It is used to eliminate toxins and restore balance in the body.

Lifestyle Recommendations: Ayurveda provides guidelines for daily routines, sleep patterns, and exercise tailored to an individual's dosha. Maintaining a harmonious lifestyle is seen as crucial for well-being.

Diagnosis and Pulse Reading: Ayurvedic practitioners employ unique diagnostic techniques, including pulse reading (Nadi Vigyan). By analyzing the pulse, they can identify imbalances and make tailored treatment recommendations.

Mind-Body Connection: Ayurveda recognizes the profound connection between the mind and the body. Emotional well-being is considered just as important as physical health, with practices like meditation and pranayama promoting mental balance.

Conclusion: Ayurveda's principles and practices offer a holistic and individualized approach to health and wellness. By understanding one's dosha, following dietary guidelines, and incorporating lifestyle recommendations, individuals can strive to achieve balance and harmony in their lives. The use of herbal medicine and detoxification therapies further enhances Ayurveda's effectiveness in preventing and treating diseases. As a system of medicine deeply rooted in ancient Indian wisdom, Ayurveda continues to find relevance and acceptance in contemporary healthcare, providing a valuable complement to modern medical practices.

TYPES OF AYURVEDIC TREATMENT AND THERAPIES

Ayurveda offers a wide range of treatment options and therapies designed to promote health and well-being. These therapies are rooted in Ayurvedic principles and aim to balance the body, mind, and spirit. In this essay, we will explore various types of Ayurvedic treatments and therapies.

Panchakarma: Panchakarma is one of the most well-known Ayurvedic therapies. It is a comprehensive detoxification process that includes five main procedures: Vamana (therapeutic vomiting), Virechana (purgation), Basti (enema), Nasya (nasal administration), and Raktamokshana (bloodletting). Panchakarma is used to eliminate toxins from the body and restore balance to the doshas.

Abhyanga: Abhyanga is the practice of Ayurvedic oil massage. Warm herbal oils are applied to the body using specific techniques. Abhyanga promotes relaxation, improves circulation, and nourishes the skin, making it a valuable therapy for overall well-being.

Shirodhara: Shirodhara involves gently pouring warm oil over the forehead in a continuous stream. This therapy is known for its profound relaxation and is often used to relieve stress, anxiety, and mental imbalances.

Swedana: Swedana refers to various types of herbal steam treatments. This therapy helps in eliminating toxins through sweat and is often used in combination with other Ayurvedic treatments.

Nasya: Nasya involves the administration of herbal oils or powders through the nostrils. It is used to treat conditions related to the head and neck, such as sinus issues and headaches.

Netra Tarpana: Netra Tarpana is an Ayurvedic therapy for the eyes. It involves creating a dough dam around the eyes and filling it with medicated ghee or oil. This therapy is used to relieve eye strain and improve vision.

Kati Basti: Kati Basti is a specialized therapy for lower back pain. A dough dam is created around the affected area, and warm herbal oil is poured into it to alleviate pain and tension.

Udvartana: Udvartana is a therapeutic dry massage that uses herbal powders. It is particularly effective for weight management, cellulite reduction, and improving circulation.

Gandusha and Kavala: These are oral therapies involving the use of herbal oils or decoctions. Gandusha is the practice of holding the liquid in the mouth, while Kavala involves gargling. These therapies promote oral health and can address issues like gum disease and bad breath.

Marma Therapy: Marma points are vital energy points in the body. Marma therapy uses gentle pressure and massage on these points to promote physical and mental well-being, as well as to alleviate pain and discomfort.

Conclusion: Ayurvedic treatments and therapies encompass a diverse range of practices, each designed to address specific health concerns and promote balance. These therapies are deeply rooted in Ayurvedic principles and offer a holistic approach to health and well-being. Whether used for detoxification, relaxation, pain relief, or the treatment of specific conditions, Ayurvedic therapies continue to be valued for their effectiveness and their ability to promote harmony in the body, mind, and spirit.

CHAPTER THREE

UNDERSTANDING FRANCHISING

HIGHLIGHTS

Franchising, a diverse business model, involves entrepreneurs (franchisees) purchasing rights from established companies (franchisors) to operate businesses, with key components like agreements, fees, and royalties, spanning various categories and types, offering advantages such as brand recognition and proven models, along with disadvantages like high initial investment and loss of autonomy; legal and regulatory aspects, both in India and internationally.

BASICS OF FRANCHISING

Franchising is a business model that has gained widespread popularity in the global marketplace. It offers a unique opportunity for entrepreneurs to own and operate their own businesses while benefiting from the support and established brand recognition of a larger corporation. This essay will delve into the basics of franchising, exploring its definition, key components, advantages, and challenges.

DEFINITION OF FRANCHISING

Franchising is a business arrangement in which an individual or entity (the franchisee) purchases the rights to operate a business using the branding, products, services, and systems of an established company (the franchisor). This agreement typically involves a contractual relationship in which the franchisor provides support, training, and ongoing assistance to the franchisee in exchange for fees, royalties, or a share of the profits.

Fig: 3.1 Depiction of Franchise network

KEY COMPONENTS OF FRANCHISING

Franchisor: The franchisor is the company that owns the established business concept and brand. They grant franchisees the right to use their intellectual property, business model, and support systems.

Franchisee: The franchisee is the individual or entity that purchases the rights to operate a business using the franchisor's brand and systems. They are responsible for running the day-to-day operations of the franchise.

Franchise Agreement: This legally binding contract outlines the terms and conditions of the franchising arrangement, including the franchisee's obligations, fees, territory, and the duration of the agreement.

Franchise Fee: The initial fee paid by the franchisee to the franchisor for the right to operate under the established brand.

Royalties: Ongoing payments made by the franchisee to the franchisor, often calculated as a percentage of the franchisee's sales.

CATEGORIES OF FRANCHISING

Franchising is a diverse business model that covers a wide range of industries and sectors. To comprehend the depth and breadth of franchising, it's crucial to examine the various categories that franchised businesses fall into. This essay explores the different categories of franchising, providing insights into the types of opportunities available to entrepreneurs and investors.

Retail Franchising: Retail franchising is one of the most common categories and involves businesses that sell products directly to consumers. This can encompass industries such as fast food, apparel, convenience stores, and automotive parts and services. In retail franchising, franchisees typically operate storefronts, adhering to the franchisor's brand standards and product offerings.

Food and Beverage Franchising: Food and beverage franchises dominate the franchising landscape, ranging from fast-food giants like McDonald's and Subway to coffee shops, ice cream parlors, and full-service restaurants. Franchisees in this category serve prepared food and beverages, benefiting from established menus, operational procedures, and brand recognition.

Service Franchising: Service-based franchises offer a wide array of services, from home cleaning and repair to health and wellness services, education, and business consulting. These franchises often provide specialized training and support to help franchisees deliver high-quality services, following the franchisor's methodologies and standards.

Hospitality Franchising: The hospitality sector includes hotels, motels, and other lodging establishments. Franchisees in this category gain access to a well-known brand, reservation systems, and support in maintaining quality standards. Hospitality franchises are prevalent globally and cater to travelers and tourists.

Automotive Franchising: Automotive franchises encompass businesses related to vehicle maintenance and repair, car rentals, and automotive accessories. Franchisees receive training and guidance on how to offer automotive services, ensuring the safety and satisfaction of their customers.

Education and Training Franchising: Education and training franchises focus on imparting knowledge and skills to students and clients. This category includes tutoring centers, language schools, and vocational training programs. Franchisees often leverage proven educational methodologies and materials.

Fitness and Wellness Franchising: In response to growing health and fitness concerns, this category has seen significant expansion. Gyms, yoga studios, and wellness centers provide franchisees with the opportunity to tap into a booming industry. They benefit from established fitness routines, equipment, and brand recognition.

Home Improvement and Renovation Franchising: Businesses in this category include home remodeling, painting, and interior design services. Franchisees receive support in managing projects, marketing their services, and maintaining quality standards, offering homeowners reliable and professional home improvement solutions.

Business Services Franchising: This category is focused on providing essential services to other businesses, such as printing, shipping, marketing, and IT support. Franchisees benefit from economies of scale and access to specialized tools and resources.

Retail Support Services: These franchises offer support services to retail businesses, including signage, logistics, and point-of-sale systems. They help franchisees streamline operations and enhance the customer experience.

Each of these categories encompasses a multitude of franchise opportunities, each with its unique advantages, challenges, and investment requirements. Potential franchisees should carefully evaluate their interests, skills, and resources to choose the category that aligns best with their goals and aspirations. Additionally, thorough research and due diligence are essential before investing in any specific franchise opportunity, ensuring that it meets their expectations and provides a path to successful entrepreneurship.

TYPES OF FRANCHISING

Franchising is a versatile business model with various approaches and types that cater to a wide range of industries and business opportunities. Understanding the different types of franchising is essential for entrepreneurs and investors seeking the right fit for their aspirations and resources. In this essay, we explore the primary types of franchising, each offering unique characteristics and opportunities.

Product Distribution Franchising: In this type of franchise, the franchisor grants the franchisee the right to distribute its products. Product distribution franchises are common in industries like soft drinks, snacks, and automotive parts. Franchisees typically operate distribution centers or delivery services to supply products to retailers or consumers within their territory.

Business Format Franchising: Business format franchising is the most well-known and prevalent type. Here, the franchisee not only uses the franchisor's products but also adopts the entire business system, including branding, operations, marketing, and support. Examples include fast-food chains, retail stores, and service-based businesses. Franchisees replicate the entire business model with guidance from the franchisor.

Manufacturing Franchising: Manufacturing franchises involve franchisees producing the franchisor's products or components using the franchisor's proprietary methods and quality standards. These products are often sold to retailers or other businesses. Manufacturing franchises are common in industries like food production and automotive manufacturing.

Single-Unit Franchising: This is the most straightforward form of franchising, where a franchisee operates a single location or unit of the franchised business. It's ideal for small-scale entrepreneurs or those who wish to test the waters of franchising before expanding further. Single-unit franchising provides localized service and often involves a lower initial investment.

Multi-Unit Franchising: Multi-unit franchising allows a franchisee to operate multiple units of the same brand in a specific territory. It's an attractive option for entrepreneurs looking to expand their franchise portfolio. This approach leverages economies of scale and can lead to significant growth. Multi-unit franchisees are responsible for managing and growing several locations.

Master Franchising (Sub-Franchising): In master franchising, a master franchisee, also known as a sub-franchisor, obtains the rights to a specific territory and acts as an intermediary between the franchisor and sub-franchisees. The master franchisee establishes and manages sub-franchise locations within their territory. This model is often used for international expansion, where local expertise is vital.

Area Development Franchising: Area development franchising grants an individual or entity the rights to develop and open a predetermined number of franchise units within a specified geographic area. This approach provides a clear growth trajectory and responsibilities for developing the brand in the region. Area developers may become multi-unit franchisees or sub-frranchisees.

Co-Operative Franchising: In co-operative franchising, franchisees join together to collectively own and operate a franchised business. This collaborative approach allows franchisees to pool resources, share responsibilities, and benefit from group decision-making. Co-operative franchises are often found in industries like agriculture, where farmers join forces to collectively market their products.

Conversion Franchising: Conversion franchising occurs when an independent business converts into a franchise under an established brand. The existing business can retain its location and customer base while receiving the support, systems, and recognition of the franchisor. This can be an attractive option for established businesses seeking to enhance their competitiveness.

Nonprofit Franchising: While less common, nonprofit organizations can also use the franchise model to expand their reach and impact. This approach is applied to charity shops, educational services, and other nonprofit ventures. The franchisees support the mission of the nonprofit and receive support in running their operations.

Each type of franchising offers distinct advantages and considerations. Entrepreneurs should carefully evaluate their goals, financial capacity, and the specific industry in which they intend to operate when selecting the right type of franchising opportunity. A well-informed decision is crucial for a successful and fulfilling journey in the world of franchising.

ADVANTAGES AND DISADVANTAGES OF FRANCHISES

Franchising is a popular business model that offers both advantages and disadvantages for entrepreneurs. Understanding these can help potential franchisees make informed decisions about whether franchising is the right path for them. Here's a breakdown of the key advantages and disadvantages of franchises:

Advantages of Franchises:

Established Brand Recognition: Franchisees benefit from operating under a well-known brand, which can lead to easier customer acquisition and trust. This brand recognition can save time and resources that would otherwise be spent on building a brand from scratch.

Proven Business Model: Franchise systems have a track record of success. The franchisor provides a proven business model, operational procedures, and marketing strategies, reducing the risk associated with starting a business from the ground up.

Training and Support: Franchisors typically provide comprehensive training programs and ongoing support, which helps franchisees understand the business and operate it effectively. This support can range from marketing assistance to operational guidance.

Economies of Scale: Franchisors often negotiate bulk purchasing discounts for supplies and inventory. This can result in cost savings for franchisees, allowing them to access resources at lower costs compared to independent businesses.

Reduced Risk: Franchising offers a lower risk compared to starting a business from scratch. The business concept is proven, which can lead to a higher likelihood of success.

Entrepreneurial Opportunities: Franchisees have the opportunity to be independent business owners while still benefiting from the structure and guidance of the franchisor. This allows individuals to experience entrepreneurship without the challenges of building a brand and business system.

Disadvantages of Franchises:

High Initial Investment: Franchisees typically need a substantial amount of capital to get started. This includes franchise fees, royalties, and other startup costs. The initial investment can be a barrier to entry for some potential entrepreneurs.

Royalty Fees and Ongoing Costs: Franchisees must pay ongoing royalties and other fees to the franchisor, often calculated as a percentage of their sales. These costs can impact profitability and add to the financial burden.

Lack of Control: Franchisees may have limited control over business decisions and operations. They must adhere to the franchisor's guidelines, which can restrict creativity and innovation. This lack of autonomy can be frustrating for some entrepreneurs.

Shared Profits: A portion of the franchisee's earnings is typically paid to the franchisor in the form of royalties or fees. This reduces the franchisee's overall profitability compared to independent business ownership.

Brand Reputation: Negative publicity or issues at other franchise locations can affect the reputation and success of all franchisees. The actions of one franchisee can impact others in the same system.

Contractual Obligations: Franchise agreements are legally binding, and breaking them can lead to legal consequences. This can limit the flexibility of franchisees to exit the system if they wish to pursue other opportunities.

In conclusion, franchises offer both advantages and disadvantages, and the decision to become a franchisee should be made after careful consideration of these factors. It's essential for potential franchisees to conduct thorough research, seek legal and financial advice, and align their goals and resources with the specific franchise opportunity they are considering. Franchising can be a rewarding path to entrepreneurship for those who understand and navigate its intricacies effectively.

LEGAL AND REGULATORY ASPECTS OF FRANCHISING IN INDIA

Franchising in India is governed by a combination of specific laws, regulations, and contractual agreements. Understanding the legal and regulatory framework is essential for both franchisors and franchisees to operate successfully and in compliance with the law. Here's an overview of the key legal and regulatory aspects of franchising in India:

Franchise Agreement: The foundation of any franchise relationship is the franchise agreement, which is a legally binding contract between the franchisor and franchisee. This agreement outlines the terms and conditions of the franchise relationship, including the rights, obligations, fees, territorial restrictions, and the duration of the agreement. It is crucial for both parties to have a clear understanding of the agreement and seek legal advice if necessary.

Indian Contract Act, 1872: Franchise agreements are contracts and are subject to the provisions of the Indian Contract Act, 1872. This act defines the legal requirements for forming a valid contract, including offer, acceptance, consideration, and the capacity of parties. It also outlines the consequences of breach of contract.

Foreign Exchange Management Act (FEMA): If the franchisor is a foreign entity, FEMA regulations come into play. These regulations govern foreign investments and the repatriation of funds. Both franchisors and franchisees should comply with FEMA guidelines when dealing with foreign exchange transactions.

Competition Law: The Competition Act, 2002, and the Competition Commission of India (CCI) regulate competition and anti-competitive practices in India. Franchisors should ensure that their franchise agreements do not include provisions that could be considered anti-competitive or monopolistic.

Intellectual Property Rights (IPR): Protecting intellectual property is vital in franchising. Trademarks, copyrights, and patents need to be registered and enforced to maintain brand integrity. The Trade Marks Act, 1999, and the Copyright Act, 1957, are key legislations related to IPR in India.

Consumer Protection Laws: The Consumer Protection Act, 2019, provides consumers with legal protections against unfair trade practices, false advertising, and substandard products or services. Franchisors must adhere to these laws to maintain consumer trust.

Taxation: India's complex taxation system can impact franchising. Income tax, goods and services tax (GST), and other taxes apply to franchise operations. Franchisees need to understand their tax obligations and maintain accurate financial records.

Retail and Commercial Leases: The rights and obligations of franchisees regarding the lease of commercial premises for the franchise business may be subject to state-specific laws. Leases are often governed by local state legislation and regulations.

Food and Safety Regulations: For franchises in the food and beverage sector, it's important to adhere to food safety and hygiene standards under the Food Safety and Standards Authority of India (FSSAI).

Licensing and Permits: Certain franchise operations may require specific licenses or permits, depending on the industry and location. For instance, health care, education, and finance-related franchises may be subject to additional regulatory requirements.

Foreign Direct Investment (FDI): If the franchise relationship involves foreign investment, it must comply with FDI regulations issued by the Indian government. These regulations dictate the sectors in which foreign investment is allowed and the limits on foreign ownership.

Navigating the legal and regulatory aspects of franchising in India can be complex. Both franchisors and franchisees are advised to seek legal counsel to ensure compliance with the applicable laws and to protect their rights and interests. Additionally, due diligence and a thorough understanding of the legal framework are essential for a successful and compliant franchise operation in India.

INTERNATIONAL LAWS FOR FRANCHISING

International laws related to franchising can vary significantly from one country to another. There isn't a single global law governing franchising, but there are some key principles and agreements that can impact franchising on an international scale:

Intellectual Property Laws: Franchising often involves the use of trademarks, patents, and other intellectual property. International intellectual property laws, including treaties like the Paris Convention and the Madrid Protocol, can play a role in protecting the rights of both the franchisor and franchisee.

Contract Law: The laws governing contracts can vary widely between countries. It's essential for franchise agreements to comply with the contract laws of both the franchisor's home country and the franchisee's home country.

Antitrust and Competition Laws: Many countries have laws that regulate anti-competitive behavior and market practices. Franchise agreements need to ensure compliance with these laws, as some arrangements can be seen as anti-competitive.

Consumer Protection Laws: Franchisees often deal with consumers, and these interactions are subject to consumer protection laws. These laws can impact pricing, disclosure requirements, and other aspects of franchising.

Foreign Investment Laws: Some countries have specific regulations regarding foreign investment, which can affect franchising, especially if a foreign franchisor is entering a new market.

Disclosure Requirements: In some countries, franchisors are required to provide detailed disclosure documents to prospective franchisees. The content and format of these documents may be regulated by law.

Dispute Resolution: International franchising agreements may specify the jurisdiction and methods for resolving disputes. International arbitration is a common method used to settle disputes between parties from different countries.

Labor Laws: Labor laws can vary widely, affecting employment practices and relationships within the franchise.

Taxation: Tax laws, including VAT and other taxes, can have significant implications for franchise arrangements. Tax planning is crucial in international franchising.

Customs and Import/Export Laws: When products or services are being imported or exported as part of the franchise, customs and trade regulations need to be considered.

It's crucial for both franchisors and franchisees to seek legal counsel with expertise in international business and franchising when establishing operations across borders. They can help navigate the specific legal requirements and ensure compliance with the laws of both the home country of the franchisor and the target market of the franchisee.

Section 2

LAYING FOUNDATION FOR FRANCHISING

CHAPTER FOUR

CHOOSE YOUR NICHE

HIGHLIGHTS

The establishment of a state-of-the-art Ayurveda hospital combines traditional Ayurvedic wisdom with modern healthcare, resulting in holistic patient care, better health outcomes, cultural preservation, and economic growth.
The takeaway is that Single Specialty Ayurveda Clinics are better because they offer specialized, personalized, and comprehensive care for specific health concerns, bridging traditional and modern medicine to promote holistic well-being.

STATE OF THE ART AYURVEDA HOSPITAL

Establishing a state-of-the-art Ayurveda hospital represents a significant step in promoting traditional healing methods while integrating modern technology and standards of healthcare. This essay explores the key aspects of setting up such a hospital, its importance, and the potential benefits it can offer to the community.

THE NEED FOR A STATE-OF-THE-ART AYURVEDA HOSPITAL

Preserving Traditional Knowledge: Ayurveda is deeply rooted in ancient Indian wisdom, with a rich history spanning thousands of years. By establishing a state-of-the-art Ayurveda hospital, we can help preserve and promote this traditional knowledge.

Holistic Healthcare: Ayurveda focuses on holistic wellness, considering the mind, body, and spirit as interconnected. Such an approach can provide a more comprehensive and patient-centered healthcare experience.

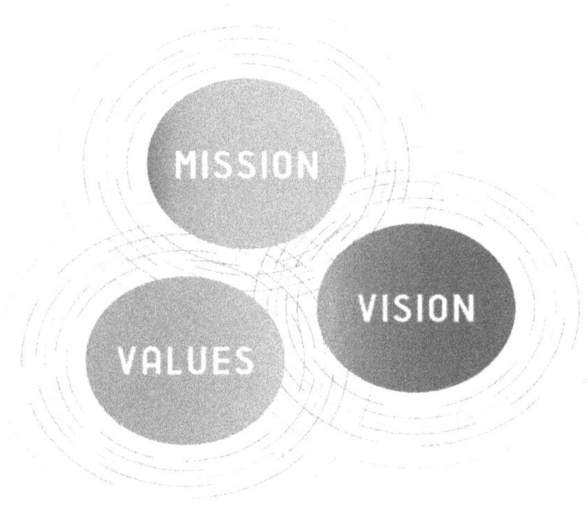

Fig: 4.1 Depiction showing mission, vision and core values

Integrating Modern Technology: Incorporating modern medical technology and infrastructure into an Ayurveda hospital ensures safety, efficiency, and precision in diagnosis and treatment, improving the overall quality of care.

Meeting Growing Demand: With the growing interest in alternative and complementary medicine, there is a rising demand for Ayurvedic treatments. A state-of-the-art Ayurveda hospital can cater to this demand effectively.

KEY COMPONENTS OF A STATE-OF-THE-ART AYURVEDA HOSPITAL

Experienced Practitioners: The cornerstone of any Ayurveda hospital is a team of experienced and skilled Ayurvedic practitioners who can provide personalized care to patients.

Research and Development: Investing in research to validate the efficacy of Ayurvedic treatments and develop new therapies is essential for the hospital's success.

Modern Infrastructure: The hospital should be equipped with state-of-the-art facilities, including diagnostic equipment, patient rooms, and treatment centers, to ensure the highest standards of healthcare.

Accreditation and Certification: Obtaining the necessary certifications and accreditations is crucial to build trust and confidence among patients and the medical community.

Patient Education: Educating patients about Ayurveda and its benefits is a vital part of the hospital's mission. Workshops, seminars, and information dissemination play a role in empowering individuals to make informed healthcare choices.

BENEFITS OF A STATE-OF-THE-ART AYURVEDA HOSPITAL

Comprehensive Care: Patients can receive integrated care that combines the strengths of Ayurveda and modern medicine for a well-rounded approach to healing.

Improved Patient Outcomes: By leveraging modern technology and research, Ayurveda can deliver even better results, addressing chronic illnesses and enhancing overall wellness.

Cultural Preservation: The hospital can contribute to the preservation of India's rich cultural heritage by promoting and nurturing Ayurvedic traditions.

Economic Growth: Establishing a state-of-the-art Ayurveda hospital can stimulate economic growth by creating jobs and promoting medical tourism.

Conclusion: The establishment of a state-of-the-art Ayurveda hospital serves as a bridge between the ancient wisdom of Ayurveda and the demands of modern healthcare. By combining traditional knowledge with modern advancements, such a hospital can provide holistic and effective healthcare while preserving the heritage of Ayurveda. It's a step toward a healthier, more informed, and culturally rich future for both the local community and the global population seeking alternative healthcare options.

SINGLE SPECIALTY AYURVEDA CLINICS

Expertise and Specialization: Single Specialty Ayurveda Clinics allow practitioners to specialize and gain expertise in specific areas of Ayurveda. This specialization enables them to provide more focused and effective treatments for patients suffering from particular ailments or conditions. For example, clinics specializing in Panchakarma can offer in-depth detoxification and rejuvenation therapies.

Tailored Treatments: Each Ayurvedic specialty clinic is designed to cater to a particular health concern, which means treatments and therapies are tailored to address those concerns. Patients can expect personalized care that aligns with their specific needs, enhancing the effectiveness of Ayurvedic treatments.

Comprehensive Care: Specialty Ayurveda clinics often provide comprehensive care by combining traditional Ayurvedic methods with modern medical practices. This integration can improve patient outcomes and offer a more holistic approach to healthcare.

TYPES OF SPECIALTY AYURVEDA CLINICS

PANCHAKARMA CLINICS

Panchakarma is a traditional Ayurvedic therapy that has been practiced for centuries in India. Panchakarma clinics are specialized centers where individuals can undergo this therapeutic process to detoxify and rejuvenate their bodies. These clinics offer a comprehensive and holistic approach to wellness, focusing on the physical, mental, and spiritual aspects of health.

The Essence of Panchakarma: Panchakarma, which means "five actions" in Sanskrit, is a set of purification and rejuvenation techniques designed to balance the body's doshas (Vata, Pitta, and Kapha) and eliminate toxins. The five primary actions of Panchakarma include Vamana (emesis), Virechana (purgation), Basti (enema), Nasya (nasal therapy), and Raktamokshana (bloodletting). These therapies are tailored to an individual's constitution and specific health concerns.

KEY COMPONENTS OF A PANCHAKARMA CLINIC

Experienced Ayurvedic Practitioners: Panchakarma clinics are staffed with skilled Ayurvedic practitioners who assess each patient's unique constitution, health history, and current imbalances. This personalized approach ensures that the Panchakarma therapies are tailored to the individual's needs.

Detoxification and Rejuvenation: The core objective of Panchakarma is to remove accumulated toxins from the body, promoting better health and vitality. This process involves a sequence of therapies, each focusing on specific detoxification mechanisms.

Dietary Guidance: Panchakarma clinics provide dietary recommendations that support the detoxification process and help maintain balance after treatment. Ayurvedic nutrition plays a crucial role in this regard, with an emphasis on wholesome, individualized diets.

Yoga and Meditation: Many Panchakarma clinics incorporate yoga and meditation practices to address the mental and spiritual dimensions of health. These techniques enhance relaxation, reduce stress, and promote overall well-being.

Herbal Medicines: Herbal remedies, formulated according to Ayurvedic principles, are often prescribed during and after Panchakarma treatment to support the body's healing process and maintain balance.

Lifestyle Counseling: Panchakarma clinics offer guidance on lifestyle adjustments that are in harmony with Ayurvedic principles. These recommendations can include daily routines, exercise, and stress management techniques.Benefits of Panchakarma: Panchakarma offers numerous benefits, including: Detoxification: Eliminating accumulated toxins and waste from the body. Improved Digestion: Enhancing digestive function and metabolism. Stress Reduction: Reducing stress and promoting mental clarity. Enhanced Immunity: Strengthening the immune system.

Chronic Disease Management: Managing chronic health conditions like arthritis, digestive disorders, and skin issues.

Conclusion: Panchakarma clinics provide a holistic approach to wellness by combining traditional Ayurvedic therapies, personalized care, and a focus on physical, mental, and spiritual well-being. This ancient practice has found relevance in modern times as people seek natural and comprehensive methods to maintain and restore their health. Panchakarma clinics are hubs of holistic healing that continue to promote balance, detoxification, and rejuvenation for individuals in pursuit of optimal well-being.

AYURVEDA DERMATOLOGY CLINICS

The Ayurveda Dermatology Clinic represents a harmonious blend of ancient Ayurvedic wisdom and modern dermatological science. It is a specialized healthcare facility where individuals can seek solutions for skin, hair, and nail-related issues while benefiting from the holistic principles of Ayurveda. This essay explores the key components and advantages of an Ayurveda Dermatology Clinic.

Foundations of Ayurveda Dermatology: Ayurveda, an ancient system of medicine originating in India, places a strong emphasis on understanding the body's constitution (Prakriti), the balance of doshas (Vata, Pitta, Kapha), and the impact of these factors on overall health. Ayurvedic dermatology is an extension of this philosophy, recognizing the intimate connection between skin health and internal imbalances.

KEY COMPONENTS OF AN AYURVEDA DERMATOLOGY CLINIC

Ayurvedic Expertise: At the heart of these clinics are Ayurvedic practitioners who are trained to diagnose skin conditions not only from a conventional dermatological standpoint but also through Ayurvedic principles. They consider doshic imbalances, digestion, lifestyle, and emotional factors that may contribute to skin issues.

Herbal Therapies: One of the cornerstones of Ayurveda Dermatology is the use of herbal remedies and formulations to address skin disorders. These natural treatments are customized to suit the unique constitution and specific skin concerns of each patient.

Diet and Lifestyle Counseling: Clinics often provide guidance on dietary modifications and lifestyle changes tailored to an individual's constitution. Such adjustments help restore balance and improve skin health from within.

Panchakarma for Skin: Panchakarma, a traditional Ayurvedic detoxification and rejuvenation therapy, can be used to treat skin issues. Procedures like Abhyanga (oil massage) and Swedana (sweating therapy) can help alleviate skin conditions by purifying the body.

Holistic Skin Care: Ayurvedic skin care is holistic, focusing on the use of natural ingredients, avoidance of harmful chemicals, and the incorporation of self-care practices. It promotes long-term skin health and beauty.

BENEFITS OF AYURVEDA DERMATOLOGY CLINICS

Holistic Approach: These clinics address skin problems at their root, considering the whole person, including mental and physical aspects, rather than merely offering topical solutions.

Personalization: Treatments are tailored to the individual's Prakriti, ensuring the best possible outcomes.

Minimal Side Effects: Ayurvedic treatments are generally safe with minimal side effects, making them suitable for a wide range of patients.

Chronic Skin Conditions: Ayurveda Dermatology can effectively manage chronic skin conditions like eczema, psoriasis, and acne, providing relief and improved quality of life.

Conclusion: The Ayurveda Dermatology Clinic represents a bridge between traditional Ayurvedic wisdom and modern dermatological science. It offers a holistic approach to skin health, emphasizing individualized care, natural remedies, and a deep understanding of the interconnectedness of skin and overall well-being. In an era where the demand for natural and personalized skin care solutions is growing, Ayurveda Dermatology Clinics provide a unique and effective approach to address a wide array of skin conditions while promoting long-term skin health and vitality.

AYURVEDA TRICHOLOGY CLINICS

The Ayurveda Trichology Clinic is a specialized healthcare facility that combines the principles of Ayurveda and trichology to address various hair and scalp-related issues. Trichology is the branch of dermatology that focuses on the study of hair and scalp health. This essay explores the key components and benefits of an Ayurveda Trichology Clinic, where traditional Ayurvedic practices are integrated with modern hair care science.

The Intersection of Ayurveda and Trichology: Ayurveda, an ancient Indian system of medicine, emphasizes a holistic approach to health, considering an individual's unique constitution (Prakriti), doshic imbalances (Vata, Pitta, Kapha), and the impact of these factors on overall well-being. Trichology, on the other hand, is a contemporary field that specializes in diagnosing and treating hair and scalp disorders using scientific methods. The Ayurveda Trichology Clinic brings these two worlds together to offer comprehensive solutions for hair and scalp health.

KEY COMPONENTS OF AN AYURVEDA TRICHOLOGY CLINIC

Ayurvedic Trichologists: The clinic is staffed with Ayurvedic trichologists who are experts in both Ayurveda and trichology. They utilize their knowledge to diagnose hair and scalp issues through an Ayurvedic lens and modern scientific techniques.

Hair and Scalp Analysis: Advanced tools and methods are used for in-depth analysis of hair and scalp conditions. This may include hair microscopy, digital imaging, and laboratory tests to identify the root causes of hair problems.

Herbal Treatments: Herbal remedies and formulations are central to Ayurvedic trichology. These natural treatments are personalized for each patient, addressing specific hair and scalp concerns while considering their unique constitution.

Lifestyle and Dietary Guidance: The clinic provides recommendations for dietary adjustments and lifestyle modifications based on Ayurvedic principles. This holistic approach helps balance internal factors that can affect hair health.

Panchakarma for Hair: Panchakarma, an Ayurvedic detoxification and rejuvenation therapy, is adapted for trichology. Procedures like Shirodhara (oil pouring on the head) and Nasya (nasal therapy) can be employed to improve scalp and hair health.

BENEFITS OF AYURVEDA TRICHOLOGY CLINICS

Personalized Care: Treatments are customized according to an individual's Prakriti, ensuring a more effective approach to hair and scalp concerns.

Natural Solutions: Ayurvedic treatments are based on natural ingredients and are free from harmful chemicals, making them suitable for a wide range of patients.

Minimal Side Effects: The treatments generally have minimal side effects, making them safer than some conventional hair care options.

Effective Management: Ayurvedic trichology can effectively manage various hair problems such as hair loss, dandruff, premature graying, and alopecia.

Conclusion: The Ayurveda Trichology Clinic is a unique and comprehensive center for addressing hair and scalp issues through the lens of both Ayurveda and trichology. It offers a holistic approach to hair care, emphasizing individualized and natural solutions for healthier hair and scalp. In a time when people seek alternatives to chemical-laden hair treatments, Ayurveda Trichology Clinics provide a bridge between ancient wisdom and modern science, focusing on long-term hair health and vitality.

AYURVEDA ORTHOPEDIC CLINICS

The Ayurveda Orthopedic Clinic represents a unique healthcare facility that blends the ancient wisdom of Ayurveda with modern orthopedic practices to treat musculoskeletal conditions. Ayurveda, a holistic Indian system of medicine, addresses the root causes of health issues, while orthopedics focuses on the diagnosis and treatment of musculoskeletal disorders. This essay explores the key components and benefits of an Ayurveda Orthopedic Clinic, where these two disciplines come together to offer comprehensive solutions for orthopedic patients.

The Fusion of Ayurveda and Orthopedics: Ayurveda places significant emphasis on understanding an individual's constitution (Prakriti), doshic imbalances (Vata, Pitta, Kapha), and the impact of these factors on health. Orthopedics, on the other hand, specializes in the diagnosis and treatment of conditions affecting the musculoskeletal system, including bones, joints, muscles, and ligaments. The Ayurveda Orthopedic Clinic bridges these two worlds to provide patients with a holistic approach to musculoskeletal health.

KEY COMPONENTS OF AN AYURVEDA ORTHOPEDIC CLINIC

Ayurvedic Orthopedic Specialists: The clinic is staffed with experts who are well-versed in both Ayurveda and orthopedics. These specialists use Ayurvedic principles to understand the underlying imbalances contributing to musculoskeletal issues.

Diagnosis and Assessment: Advanced diagnostic tools, including X-rays, MRIs, and other imaging techniques, are utilized to accurately diagnose musculoskeletal conditions. Ayurvedic assessments are integrated to provide a holistic view of the patient's health.

Herbal Remedies: Ayurvedic herbal treatments and formulations are central to the clinic's approach. These natural therapies are customized to address the specific musculoskeletal concerns of each patient while considering their unique constitution.

Lifestyle and Dietary Guidance: The clinic provides recommendations for lifestyle modifications and dietary changes based on Ayurvedic principles. These adjustments help restore balance and promote overall well-being, which is crucial for musculoskeletal health.

Panchakarma for Orthopedics: Panchakarma, an Ayurvedic detoxification and rejuvenation therapy, is adapted for orthopedic patients. Procedures like Abhyanga (oil massage) and Swedana (sweating therapy) can be employed to improve musculoskeletal health.

BENEFITS OF AYURVEDA ORTHOPEDIC CLINICS

Holistic Care: These clinics offer a more comprehensive approach to musculoskeletal issues by addressing the root causes and promoting overall health.

Personalized Treatments: Ayurvedic treatments are tailored to an individual's Prakriti, ensuring a more effective approach to orthopedic concerns.

Natural Solutions: Ayurvedic remedies are based on natural ingredients and are generally free from harmful chemicals, making them suitable for a wide range of patients.

Effective Management: Ayurveda Orthopedic Clinics can effectively manage musculoskeletal conditions such as arthritis, back pain, joint issues, and sports injuries.

Conclusion: The Ayurveda Orthopedic Clinic is a unique and valuable resource for individuals seeking holistic solutions for musculoskeletal issues. By combining the principles of Ayurveda and modern orthopedic care, these clinics offer a bridge between ancient wisdom and contemporary medical science. In an era where many patients seek natural and individualized approaches to orthopedic concerns, Ayurveda Orthopedic Clinics provide a comprehensive strategy for restoring musculoskeletal health, promoting well-being, and managing conditions more effectively.

AYURVEDA GYNAECOLOGY CLINICS

The Ayurveda Gynaecology Clinic is a specialized healthcare facility dedicated to addressing women's health concerns using the principles of Ayurveda. Ayurveda, an ancient Indian system of medicine, emphasizes a holistic approach to health and wellness. In the context of gynaecology, Ayurveda offers unique insights and natural treatments for a wide range of women's health issues. This essay explores the key components and advantages of an Ayurveda Gynaecology Clinic, where traditional Ayurvedic practices are integrated with modern gynaecological care.

The Intersection of Ayurveda and Gynaecology: Ayurveda recognizes the unique physiological and emotional aspects of women's health and provides an integrated approach to gynaecology. It takes into consideration an individual's constitution (Prakriti), doshic imbalances (Vata, Pitta, Kapha), and the impact of these factors on women's health. By combining the wisdom of Ayurveda with gynaecological expertise, the Ayurveda Gynaecology Clinic offers a holistic approach to women's well-being.

KEY COMPONENTS OF AN AYURVEDA GYNAECOLOGY CLINIC

Ayurvedic Gynaecologists: The clinic is staffed with Ayurvedic gynaecologists who are experts in both Ayurveda and women's health. They use Ayurvedic principles to diagnose and treat gynaecological conditions, including menstrual disorders, fertility issues, and menopausal symptoms.

Herbal Therapies: Herbal remedies and formulations are central to the clinic's approach. These natural treatments are personalized for each patient, addressing specific gynaecological concerns while considering their unique constitution.

Dietary and Lifestyle Guidance: The clinic provides recommendations for dietary adjustments and lifestyle modifications based on Ayurvedic principles. These adjustments help balance internal factors that can affect women's health, such as hormonal imbalances.

Panchakarma for Women: Panchakarma, an Ayurvedic detoxification and rejuvenation therapy, is adapted for women's health. Procedures like Abhyanga (oil massage) and Yoni Pichu (vaginal oil therapy) can be employed to improve gynaecological well-being.

Holistic Women's Health Care: The clinic offers holistic women's health care, which includes the promotion of mental and emotional well-being. Techniques such as yoga and meditation are often integrated into treatment plans.

BENEFITS OF AYURVEDA GYNAECOLOGY CLINICS

Holistic Care: These clinics offer a more comprehensive approach to women's health by addressing the root causes of gynaecological issues and promoting overall well-being.

Personalized Treatments: Ayurvedic treatments are tailored to an individual's Prakriti, ensuring a more effective approach to gynaecological concerns.

Natural Solutions: Ayurvedic remedies are based on natural ingredients and are generally free from harmful chemicals, making them suitable for a wide range of patients.

Effective Management: Ayurveda Gynaecology Clinics can effectively manage conditions such as menstrual irregularities, polycystic ovarian syndrome (PCOS), and menopausal symptoms.

Conclusion: The Ayurveda Gynaecology Clinic serves as a bridge between traditional Ayurvedic wisdom and modern gynaecological care. It offers a holistic approach to women's health, emphasizing individualized and natural solutions for a wide range of gynaecological concerns. In an era where women increasingly seek natural and personalized approaches to women's health, Ayurveda Gynaecology Clinics provide a comprehensive strategy for promoting and maintaining women's well-being throughout their life stages.

AYURVEDA MENTAL HEALTH CLINICS

The Ayurveda Mental Health Clinic is a specialized healthcare facility that marries the ancient principles of Ayurveda with contemporary mental health care. Ayurveda, a traditional Indian system of medicine, focuses on the holistic well-being of individuals. In the context of mental health, Ayurveda offers a unique approach to understanding and addressing psychological issues. This essay explores the key components and advantages of an Ayurveda Mental Health Clinic, where traditional Ayurvedic practices are integrated with modern mental health care.

The Intersection of Ayurveda and Mental Health: Ayurveda recognizes the intricate connection between the mind and body and considers the doshas (Vata, Pitta, Kapha) when assessing an individual's mental health. Mental well-being is seen as a reflection of the balance and harmony of these doshas, as well as the state of the mind. By combining the wisdom of Ayurveda with modern psychology and psychiatry, Ayurveda Mental Health Clinics provide a holistic approach to mental health.

KEY COMPONENTS OF AN AYURVEDA MENTAL HEALTH CLINIC

Ayurvedic Mental Health Specialists: The clinic is staffed with professionals who are experts in both Ayurveda and mental health. These specialists use Ayurvedic principles to diagnose and treat mental health conditions, including stress, anxiety, depression, and mood disorders.

Herbal Therapies: Herbal remedies and formulations are central to the clinic's approach. These natural treatments are personalized for each patient, addressing specific mental health concerns while considering their unique constitution.

Dietary and Lifestyle Guidance: The clinic provides recommendations for dietary adjustments and lifestyle modifications based on Ayurvedic principles. These adjustments help balance internal factors that can affect mental well-being, including diet and daily routines.

Panchakarma for Mental Health: Panchakarma, an Ayurvedic detoxification and rejuvenation therapy, is adapted for mental health. Procedures like Shirodhara (oil pouring on the head) and Nasya (nasal therapy) can be employed to improve mental well-being and reduce stress.

Holistic Mental Health Care: The clinic offers holistic mental health care that emphasizes not only psychological well-being but also emotional and spiritual balance. Techniques such as yoga and meditation are often integrated into treatment plans.

BENEFITS OF AYURVEDA MENTAL HEALTH CLINICS

Holistic Care: These clinics offer a more comprehensive approach to mental health by addressing the root causes of psychological issues and promoting overall well-being.

Personalized Treatments: Ayurvedic treatments are tailored to an individual's constitution (Prakriti) and doshic imbalances, ensuring a more effective approach to mental health concerns.

Natural Solutions: Ayurvedic remedies are based on natural ingredients and are generally free from harmful chemicals, making them suitable for a wide range of patients.

Effective Management: Ayurveda Mental Health Clinics can effectively manage mental health conditions, providing relief and improved quality of life for those suffering from stress, anxiety, depression, and related disorders.

Conclusion: The Ayurveda Mental Health Clinic serves as a bridge between traditional Ayurvedic wisdom and modern mental health care. It offers a holistic approach to mental health, emphasizing individualized and natural solutions for a wide range of psychological concerns. In an era where individuals seek natural and personalized approaches to mental health, Ayurveda Mental Health Clinics provide a comprehensive strategy for promoting and maintaining psychological well-being and harmony in the modern world.

AYURVEDA DIGESTIVE HEALTH CLINICS

The Ayurveda Digestive Health Clinic is a specialized healthcare facility that blends the profound insights of Ayurveda with modern digestive health practices. Ayurveda, a traditional Indian system of medicine, emphasizes holistic wellness and considers the digestive system as the foundation of overall health. This essay delves into the key components and benefits of an Ayurveda Digestive Health Clinic, where ancient Ayurvedic principles are harmoniously integrated with contemporary digestive care.

The Marriage of Ayurveda and Digestive Health: Ayurveda recognizes the critical role of digestion in maintaining overall health and well-being. It assesses an individual's constitution (Prakriti), doshic imbalances (Vata, Pitta, Kapha), and dietary habits to understand and address digestive issues. By combining the wisdom of Ayurveda with modern digestive care, the Ayurveda Digestive Health Clinic offers a holistic approach to digestive well-being.

KEY COMPONENTS OF AN AYURVEDA DIGESTIVE HEALTH CLINIC

Ayurvedic Digestive Health Specialists: The clinic employs professionals well-versed in both Ayurveda and digestive health. These experts use Ayurvedic principles to diagnose and treat digestive disorders, including irritable bowel syndrome (IBS), acid reflux, and food sensitivities.

Herbal Remedies: Herbal treatments and formulations are central to the clinic's approach. These natural therapies are tailored for each patient, addressing specific digestive concerns while considering their unique constitution and doshic imbalances.

Dietary and Lifestyle Guidance: The clinic provides recommendations for dietary adjustments and lifestyle modifications based on Ayurvedic principles. These changes help restore balance and promote overall well-being, particularly with regard to digestive health.

Panchakarma for Digestive Health: Panchakarma, an Ayurvedic detoxification and rejuvenation therapy, is adapted for digestive health. Procedures like Virechana (purgation) and Basti (enema) can be employed to cleanse and revitalize the digestive system.

Holistic Digestive Wellness: The clinic emphasizes holistic digestive health, incorporating mindfulness techniques, stress management, and yoga to promote mental and emotional well-being alongside physical wellness.

BENEFITS OF AYURVEDA DIGESTIVE HEALTH CLINICS

Comprehensive Care: These clinics offer a more comprehensive approach to digestive health by addressing the root causes of digestive issues and promoting overall well-being.

Personalized Treatments: Ayurvedic treatments are tailored to an individual's constitution and doshic imbalances, ensuring a more effective approach to digestive concerns.

Natural Solutions: Ayurvedic remedies are based on natural ingredients and are typically free from harmful chemicals, making them suitable for a wide range of patients.

Effective Management: Ayurveda Digestive Health Clinics can effectively manage digestive conditions, providing relief for individuals dealing with a range of issues, from indigestion to chronic gastrointestinal disorders.

Conclusion: The Ayurveda Digestive Health Clinic acts as a bridge between traditional Ayurvedic wisdom and modern digestive health care. It offers a holistic approach to digestive well-being, emphasizing individualized and natural solutions for various digestive concerns. In a world where individuals are increasingly seeking natural and personalized approaches to digestive health, Ayurveda Digestive Health Clinics provide a comprehensive strategy for promoting and maintaining digestive wellness, vital for overall health and vitality

AYURVEDIC WEIGHT MANAGEMENT CLINICS

Ayurveda, one of the world's oldest holistic healing systems, has gained significant recognition for its natural and holistic approach to weight management. Ayurvedic weight management clinics offer individuals a unique blend of ancient wisdom and modern science to address the rising concern of obesity and its related health issues. This essay explores the principles, treatments, and benefits of Ayurvedic weight management clinics.

THE PRINCIPLES OF AYURVEDIC WEIGHT MANAGEMENT

Individual Constitution (Prakriti): Ayurveda identifies three main body types, or doshas (Vata, Pitta, and Kapha). Each person has a unique constitution, and Ayurvedic weight management considers the individual's dosha when devising a personalized plan.

Balance of Doshas: The imbalance of doshas is often at the root of weight gain. Ayurvedic practitioners aim to restore this balance through dietary and lifestyle changes, along with herbal remedies.

Mind-Body Connection: Ayurveda recognizes the strong connection between mental and physical health. Stress, emotional imbalances, and poor lifestyle choices can lead to weight gain. Ayurvedic treatments address these factors.

TREATMENTS OFFERED IN AYURVEDIC WEIGHT MANAGEMENT CLINICS

Dietary Guidance: Ayurvedic experts prescribe personalized diets that align with an individual's dosha. This often includes a focus on whole, unprocessed foods and mindful eating practices.

Herbal Supplements: Natural herbs and remedies are used to support metabolism, digestion, and detoxification. These are carefully chosen to suit the person's constitution.

Lifestyle Modifications: Ayurvedic clinics emphasize the importance of daily routines (dinacharya) and seasonal routines (ritucharya) to promote wellness. These routines can include exercise, yoga, meditation, and adequate sleep.

Detoxification (Panchakarma): Panchakarma is a detoxification process that includes therapies like oil massages, herbal steam baths, and cleansing enemas. It helps remove toxins from the body and balance the doshas.

BENEFITS OF AYURVEDIC WEIGHT MANAGEMENT CLINICS

Sustainable Weight Loss: Ayurveda focuses on long-term lifestyle changes rather than quick fixes, making weight loss more sustainable.

Holistic Health Improvement: Ayurvedic treatments not only help with weight management but also enhance overall well-being by addressing the root causes of health issues.

Personalized Approach: By considering an individual's constitution, Ayurvedic clinics provide customized solutions, which can be more effective than one-size-fits-all approaches.

Natural and Safe: Ayurvedic treatments primarily rely on natural herbs and therapies, minimizing the risk of side effects often associated with pharmaceutical interventions.

Stress Reduction: Ayurveda emphasizes stress management, which can be a significant factor in weight gain. Stress reduction techniques lead to better mental health.

Conclusion: Ayurvedic weight management clinics offer a holistic and time-tested approach to weight management that prioritizes individualized care and overall well-being. While Ayurveda's effectiveness may vary from person to person, it provides an alternative path for those seeking a natural, balanced, and sustainable approach to weight loss and improved health. As the world grapples with the challenges of obesity and its related health problems, Ayurvedic weight management clinics stand as an ancient yet relevant solution.

AYURVEDA BEAUTY CLINICS

In the pursuit of beauty and well-being, many individuals are turning to Ayurveda Beauty Clinics as a holistic alternative to conventional beauty treatments. Ayurveda, an ancient system of medicine originating in India, places a strong emphasis on the interconnectedness of mind, body, and spirit. Ayurveda Beauty Clinics offer a unique approach to beauty that goes beyond superficial treatments and focuses on promoting overall health and balance. This essay explores the concept of Ayurveda Beauty Clinics, their principles, services, and the benefits they offer.

SERVICES OFFERED BY AYURVEDA BEAUTY CLINICS

Ayurveda Beauty Clinics provide a range of services that align with the principles of Ayurveda. These services are designed to restore balance and enhance an individual's natural beauty. Some common services offered include:

Ayurvedic Skin Care: Customized skincare treatments that use natural ingredients and herbal formulations to address skin issues and promote a healthy complexion.

Ayurvedic Hair Care: Hair treatments that focus on nourishing the scalp and hair, using herbs and oils to maintain healthy and lustrous locks.

Ayurvedic Massages: Therapeutic massages that use herbal oils to relax the body, reduce stress, and improve circulation, which indirectly enhances the skin's radiance.

Diet and Nutrition: Ayurvedic clinics often provide dietary recommendations based on an individual's dosha, ensuring that nutrition supports overall health and beauty.

Stress Reduction: Stress management techniques, including yoga and meditation, to achieve mental peace and emotional balance, which are considered essential for beauty.

BENEFITS OF AYURVEDA BEAUTY CLINICS

The Ayurveda Beauty Clinic approach to beauty offers several benefits:

Natural and Safe: Ayurvedic treatments rely on natural ingredients and holistic approaches, minimizing the use of chemicals and synthetic products that may have adverse effects on the skin and body.

Balanced Beauty: Rather than focusing solely on superficial aspects, Ayurveda Beauty Clinics address the root causes of beauty issues by promoting balance and well-being.

Customization: Treatments are personalized based on an individual's dosha and specific needs, ensuring that they are effective and harmonious.

Long-Lasting Results: Ayurvedic beauty treatments aim for lasting results by addressing the underlying imbalances in the body.

Stress Reduction: The incorporation of stress-reduction techniques improves mental well-being, which is closely linked to an individual's appearance.

Conclusion: Ayurveda Beauty Clinics represent a holistic and well-rounded approach to beauty and well-being. In a world where cosmetic enhancements and quick fixes are prevalent, Ayurveda offers an alternative that focuses on long-term health and balanced beauty. By embracing the principles of Ayurveda and the services provided by these clinics, individuals can find an avenue to enhance their natural beauty while promoting physical and mental harmony. In essence, Ayurveda Beauty Clinics are a reflection of the age-old wisdom that true beauty radiates from the inside out.

AYURVEDA SPA AND WELLNESS CENTRE

Ayurveda Spa and Wellness Centres have emerged as sanctuaries where individuals seek solace and healing through the profound wisdom of Ayurvedic practices. This essay delves into the concept, offerings, and significance of Ayurveda Spa and Wellness Centres.

THE ESSENCE OF AYURVEDA SPA AND WELLNESS

Ayurveda Spa and Wellness Centres are places of rejuvenation and healing that blend traditional Ayurvedic principles with modern amenities. At their core, these centers aim to restore and maintain harmony within the individual. They recognize that well-being is not merely the absence of disease but a balanced state of physical, mental, and emotional health. Here's a closer look at what these centers offer:

Ayurvedic Therapies: The heart of Ayurveda Spa and Wellness Centres lies in the therapeutic treatments derived from ancient Ayurvedic texts. These treatments, which include Abhyanga (oil massage), Shirodhara (oil pouring on the forehead), and Panchakarma (detoxification), are tailored to individual doshas (biological energies) to restore equilibrium.

Mind-Body Connection: Ayurveda places a strong emphasis on the mind-body connection. These centers often provide yoga and meditation classes to promote mental and emotional well-being. Guests can learn techniques to manage stress, enhance focus, and cultivate a tranquil mind.

Nutrition: Proper nutrition is a fundamental aspect of Ayurveda. Guests are guided in understanding their unique dietary needs based on their dosha, and wholesome Ayurvedic meals are served to nourish and balance the body.

Holistic Healing: Beyond physical health, Ayurveda Spa and Wellness Centres focus on overall wellness. They offer lifestyle counseling, personalized wellness plans, and herbal remedies to address various health concerns and maintain a balanced life.

Significance of Ayurveda Spa and Wellness Centres

The significance of Ayurveda Spa and Wellness Centres extends far beyond relaxation and rejuvenation. They serve as essential bridges between ancient wisdom and modern health needs:

Holistic Approach: Ayurveda takes a holistic approach to health, which aligns with the growing interest in holistic medicine and preventive healthcare worldwide. These centers offer an alternative to conventional medical practices by addressing the root causes of health issues.

Cultural Preservation: Ayurveda Spa and Wellness Centres contribute to the preservation of traditional knowledge and culture. They encourage the use of herbal remedies, Ayurvedic principles, and yoga, keeping these ancient practices alive and relevant.

Stress Management: In today's fast-paced world, stress and its associated health problems are prevalent. These centers offer effective stress management techniques, helping individuals cope with the demands of modern life.

Personalized Care: Ayurveda recognizes that each person is unique, and wellness should be tailored to individual needs. These centers provide personalized care, focusing on the individual's specific constitution and health goals.

CHAPTER FIVE

DEVELOPING AN AYURVEDA BUSINESS CONCEPT

HIGHLIGHTS

Crafting a robust documentation framework for an Ayurveda clinic franchise, covering essential aspects such as franchise agreements, operations manuals, branding guidelines, compliance, financial reporting, training, and site setup, is imperative for ensuring consistency, quality, and success in the expansion of the business model.

MAKE A BUSINESS PLAN
SWOT ANALYSIS OF AYURVEDA CLINIC

To perform a SWOT analysis for your Ayurveda clinic, you'll need to assess its internal strengths and weaknesses as well as external opportunities and threats. Here's a step-by-step guide:

Identify Strengths (S):

Consider what your clinic excels at in comparison to others. This could be the expertise of your Ayurvedic practitioners, a strong reputation, a unique treatment approach, or a convenient location.

Think about your clinic's resources, such as well-equipped facilities, a skilled support staff, or a loyal customer base.

Identify Weaknesses (W):

Assess areas where your clinic falls short. This might include limited marketing efforts, outdated equipment, staff shortages, or challenges in offering certain treatments.

Consider customer feedback and complaints to identify weaknesses in customer service or treatment outcomes.

Identify Opportunities (O):

Examine the external factors that could benefit your clinic. These may include a growing interest in holistic healthcare, partnerships with other healthcare providers, or the potential to expand your services.

Look for emerging trends in Ayurveda or integrative medicine.

Identify Threats (T):

Identify external factors that could pose a threat to your clinic's success. This might include competition from other healthcare providers, regulatory changes, economic downturns, or negative public perceptions of Ayurveda.

Consider the impact of changing healthcare policies or insurance coverage on your clinic's revenue.

Fig:5.1 Image showing copy of Franchise agreement

Prioritize and Analyze: Once you have identified the SWOT factors, prioritize them based on their significance and potential impact.

Analyze how you can leverage your strengths to seize opportunities, address weaknesses to mitigate threats, or turn weaknesses into strengths.

Develop Strategies: Create strategies to capitalize on your strengths and opportunities. For example, if your clinic has a strong reputation (S), you can market it as a trusted Ayurvedic center (O).

Develop plans to address weaknesses and threats, such as investing in staff training (W) to improve service quality and meet changing healthcare regulations (T).

Implementation and Monitoring: Put your strategies into action and monitor their effectiveness regularly. Adjust your strategies as needed based on ongoing evaluations.

Remember that a SWOT analysis is a dynamic process and should be revisited periodically to adapt to changing circumstances in the healthcare industry and your clinic's operations.

FEASIBILITY TEST FOR AN AYURVEDA CLINIC FOR FRANCHISING

When conducting a feasibility test for franchising an Ayurveda clinic, you'll need to assess various aspects to ensure the viability and success of this expansion. Here's a more specific guide tailored to the Ayurveda clinic franchising scenario:

Market Analysis: Assess the demand for Ayurvedic services in potential franchise locations. Analyze demographics, healthcare trends, and competition.

Identify the target audience and their acceptance of Ayurveda in those areas.

Franchise Model: Define the structure of your franchise model (single-unit, multi-unit, master franchise, etc.). Determine franchise fees, royalty structure, and support services you'll offer to franchisees.

Legal and Regulatory Considerations: Understand and comply with legal and healthcare regulations for operating Ayurveda clinics in various locations. Ensure that your franchise model aligns with franchise and healthcare laws.

Costs and Investment: Calculate the initial investment required for each franchise, including licensing fees, clinic setup, equipment, staff hiring and training, and marketing expenses. Develop financial projections to estimate the potential return on investment for franchisees.

Franchisee Selection: Define criteria for selecting franchisees. Look for individuals with the right qualifications, commitment, and alignment with your brand's values.

Support and Training: Develop a comprehensive training program for franchisees and their staff. Provide ongoing support and resources to ensure the success of franchisees.

Brand and Marketing: Establish a strong brand identity that can be replicated by franchisees. Develop a marketing strategy that maintains brand consistency across multiple locations.

Operational Systems: Document standard operating procedures (SOPs) for clinic operations, covering patient care, appointment scheduling, inventory management, financial reporting, and other critical processes.

Financial Projections: Create detailed financial projections for the franchise business, including revenue, expenses, and profitability over a set timeframe.

Franchise Agreement: Develop a comprehensive franchise agreement that outlines the rights and responsibilities of both the franchisor and franchisees.

Risk Assessment: Identify potential risks and challenges associated with franchising, such as market saturation, competition, and changing healthcare regulations. Develop strategies to mitigate these risks.

Pilot Testing: Consider piloting the franchise model in a single location to test its viability and make necessary adjustments before expanding further.

Legal and Financial Advisors: Consult with legal and financial advisors who specialize in franchising to ensure compliance with all legal and financial aspects.

Feasibility Report: Compile the findings of your feasibility study into a comprehensive report that includes all the above factors.

Decision Making: Based on the feasibility study, make an informed decision on whether to proceed with franchising your Ayurveda clinic. A thorough feasibility test is essential to assess the potential success and sustainability of the franchise network. It will help you make an informed decision and establish a strong foundation for franchising your Ayurveda clinic.

MARKET RESEARCH AND COMPETITIVE ANALYSIS

Market research and competitive analysis are indispensable tools for businesses seeking to thrive in today's dynamic and competitive landscape. These practices provide valuable insights into consumer behavior, industry trends, and the strategies of rivals. In this essay, we will explore the significance of market research and competitive analysis, as well as their role in shaping informed decision-making for businesses.

Market Research: Market research is the systematic gathering, analysis, and interpretation of data about a specific market, including its potential customers, competitors, and various external factors. This process yields valuable information that can guide a company's product development, marketing strategies, and overall business operations.

Understanding Consumer Behavior: Market research helps in comprehending consumer preferences, buying patterns, and evolving trends. It enables businesses to tailor their products and services to better meet customer needs. For example, a clothing retailer may use market research to identify popular fashion trends and stock their inventory accordingly.

Identifying Market Gaps: By conducting market research, companies can uncover unmet needs or underserved market segments. This information can lead to innovative product or service offerings. Airbnb, for instance, identified a gap in the hospitality industry by connecting travelers with unique, affordable accommodations.

Assessing Market Size and Potential: Market research allows businesses to estimate the size of their target market and evaluate its growth potential. This information is essential for strategic planning and investment decisions.

Competitive Analysis: Competitive analysis is the process of assessing and understanding the strengths and weaknesses of competitors in the same industry. It involves studying their strategies, products, market positioning, and customer base.

Identifying Key Competitors: Competitive analysis helps companies identify their primary competitors, both direct and indirect. This knowledge is crucial for positioning and differentiating the company's offerings effectively.

Learning from Competitors: By studying the strategies and successes of competitors, businesses can gain insights into what works in the market. For instance, fast-food chains often adapt successful menu items from their rivals.

Strategic Decision-Making: Competitive analysis informs important strategic decisions, such as pricing, marketing, and product development. It allows a company to respond to changes in the competitive landscape swiftly. Synergy between Market Research and Competitive Analysis Market research and competitive analysis are closely intertwined and complement each other in several ways.

Market Dynamics: Competitive analysis helps companies understand the dynamics of the industry by shedding light on how competitors adapt to market changes. Market research, on the other hand, provides insights into customer behavior and preferences that can be leveraged strategically.

Identifying Opportunities and Threats: When conducted together, these practices help businesses identify opportunities to exploit and threats to mitigate. By analyzing both the market and competitors, companies can make informed decisions that align with their strengths and market realities.

Sustainable Growth: The synergy between market research and competitive analysis is essential for achieving sustainable growth. A business that effectively combines these practices can adapt to changing market conditions and maintain a competitive edge over time.

Conclusion

Market research and competitive analysis are invaluable tools for businesses seeking to make informed, data-driven decisions in an increasingly complex and competitive business environment. Together, they provide a comprehensive understanding of the market landscape, customer behavior, and the competitive field. This knowledge empowers businesses to develop strategies that are more likely to succeed, differentiate themselves from competitors, and ultimately thrive in the marketplace. In a world where knowledge is power, market research and competitive analysis are the keys to unlocking success.

HERE'S AN OUTLINE FOR A BUSINESS PLAN FOR AN AYURVEDA FRANCHISE CLINIC:

1. Executive Summary:
Briefly describe the clinic's mission and vision.
Provide an overview of the franchise model and its unique selling points.
Summarize the financial requirements and potential returns.

2. Business Description:
Explain the concept of the Ayurveda clinic and its services.
Detail the background and history of Ayurveda.
Highlight the unique features of your franchise clinic.

3. Market Analysis:
Define the target market (demographics, location, etc.).
Analyze the demand for Ayurvedic services in the chosen area.
Research competitors and their strengths and weaknesses.

4. Organization and Management:
Outline the organizational structure and management team.
Provide bios for key team members and their roles.
Describe the franchise support and training provided.

5. Services and Products:
List the Ayurvedic services and products offered.
Explain the quality and sourcing of products.
Discuss any unique treatment protocols or therapies.

6. Marketing and Sales Strategy:
Explain how you'll market the clinic locally.
Outline a digital marketing strategy.
Detail sales and promotion tactics.

7. Funding Requirements:
Specify the initial investment required for the franchise.
Detail ongoing operational costs.
Discuss financing options, if applicable.
8. Financial Projections:
Present a detailed financial forecast for the next 3-5 years.
Include income statements, balance sheets, and cash flow projections.
Highlight break-even points and ROI.

9. Franchisee Support:
Describe the training and support provided to franchisees.
Explain the terms and conditions of the franchise agreement.
Address ongoing support and communication channels.

10. Legal and Compliance:
Outline any legal requirements for the clinic.
Discuss intellectual property rights and branding.
Explain any certifications or licenses needed.

11. Risk Assessment:
Identify potential risks and challenges.
Explain how these risks will be mitigated.
Highlight contingency plans.

12. Appendix:
Include any additional documents, such as market research, legal agreements, or detailed financial spreadsheets.

Remember, the specific details will vary based on the Ayurveda franchise you're considering, the location, and other unique factors. It's essential to conduct thorough research and customization for your specific business plan

Developing a successful Ayurveda business concept requires a deep understanding of the principles of Ayurveda, market research, a clear vision, and a well-structured plan.

Before embarking on an Ayurveda business venture, it is essential to have a comprehensive understanding of Ayurveda. Ayurveda is founded on the principles of balance, harmony, and individualization. It classifies people into distinct body types or doshas (Vata, Pitta, and Kapha) and prescribes treatments, diets, and lifestyle choices based on these doshas. To run a successful Ayurveda business, you need a strong grasp of these concepts and a commitment to adhering to the holistic philosophy of Ayurveda.

Market Research: Market research is a crucial step in developing an Ayurveda business concept. Begin by identifying your target audience and understanding their needs and preferences. Assess the demand for Ayurvedic products and services in your region or target market. Competitor analysis is equally important; study existing Ayurveda businesses to identify gaps in the market or areas where you can differentiate your business.

Business Concept: Your Ayurveda business concept should be well-defined and unique. Consider the following aspects:

Services: Determine whether you want to offer Ayurvedic consultations, therapies, herbal products, or a combination of these. Decide if you will focus on preventive wellness, holistic healing, or a specific niche within Ayurveda.

Location: Choose a suitable location for your business, whether it's a wellness center, spa, clinic, or an online platform. The location should align with your target audience.

Branding: Develop a compelling brand that reflects the values and philosophy of Ayurveda. The branding should resonate with your target audience and set you apart from competitors.

Team: Recruit trained Ayurvedic practitioners and therapists. Ensure they have the necessary certifications and a deep understanding of Ayurvedic principles.

Products: If you plan to sell Ayurvedic products, source or develop high-quality, authentic herbal formulations that are in line with Ayurvedic principles.

Regulations and Compliance: It's essential to understand and comply with local regulations and certifications related to Ayurveda. Depending on your location, there may be specific guidelines for Ayurveda businesses, especially when it comes to the practice of medicine and the sale of herbal products. Ensure that your business adheres to all legal requirements.

Marketing and Promotion: Create a marketing strategy that effectively reaches your target audience. Consider using a combination of online and offline marketing channels, including a professional website, social media, content marketing, and collaborations with other wellness providers. Educate your audience about the benefits of Ayurveda and how your business can meet their health and wellness needs.

Conclusion: Developing an Ayurveda business concept is a journey that requires a strong foundation in Ayurvedic principles, thorough market research, a well-defined concept, compliance with regulations, and an effective marketing strategy. By combining a deep respect for Ayurveda's holistic philosophy with a unique and well-executed business plan, entrepreneurs can tap into the growing demand for natural and holistic healthcare solutions while promoting the principles of balance and well-being.

Write Mission, Vision, and Core Values: Guiding Principles for Success Mission, vision, and core values are fundamental elements that shape the identity and direction of an organization. They provide a strategic framework that guides decision-making, inspires employees, and communicates the organization's purpose to stakeholders. This essay explores the significance of mission, vision, and core values in both for-profit and nonprofit settings, highlighting their role in achieving long-term success.

Mission Statement: A mission statement serves as an organization's north star, encapsulating its reason for existence and the primary goals it seeks to achieve. It defines what the organization does, who it serves, and how it does it. A well-crafted mission statement is clear, concise, and inspirational, motivating employees to work towards a common purpose. For example, Google's mission is "to organize the world's information and make it universally accessible and useful." This mission guides its activities in technology, information retrieval, and digital services.

Vision Statement: While the mission statement addresses the present, the vision statement looks to the future. It paints a vivid picture of what the organization aspires to become and the impact it seeks to make in the long term. An effective vision statement inspires innovation, sets ambitious goals, and provides direction for strategic planning. Tesla's vision to "create the most compelling car company of the 21st century" not only outlines its aspirations but also motivates employees to push the boundaries of electric vehicle technology.

Core Values: Core values represent an organization's fundamental beliefs and principles. They guide the behavior of employees, shape the culture, and dictate decision-making. Core values are the moral compass of an organization, defining what it stands for and what it will not compromise. Apple's core values include innovation, simplicity, and excellence. These values inform product design, customer service, and the company's overall approach to business.

Importance and Implementation: The importance of mission, vision, and core values cannot be overstated. They provide clarity, alignment, and a sense of purpose within an organization. A strong mission statement ensures that everyone understands why the organization exists. A compelling vision statement inspires employees and stakeholders to work together towards a shared future. Core values, when lived and upheld, create a positive and ethical work environment.

To implement these principles effectively, leadership plays a critical role. The leaders are responsible for articulating and embodying the organization's mission and values. They must lead by example, fostering a culture that aligns with the stated principles. Additionally, these elements should be integrated into strategic planning, decision-making processes, and performance evaluations to ensure that the organization remains true to its mission, works toward its vision, and upholds its core values.

Conclusion: In conclusion, mission, vision, and core values are essential components of any organization's identity and strategy. They provide a sense of purpose, direction, and a framework for decision-making. When crafted and implemented effectively, these elements can serve as powerful tools for success, guiding an organization towards achieving its goals, inspiring its employees, and building a positive reputation with stakeholders. In a constantly changing and competitive world, a well-defined mission, a compelling vision, and strong core values become a source of stability and strength.

DOCUMENTATION FOR AYURVEDA CLINIC FRANCHISE

Creating documentation for an Ayurveda clinic franchise involves several key components. Here's an outline to get you started:

Franchise Agreement:

Define the terms and conditions of the franchise relationship.

Specify the franchise fees, royalties, and other financial obligations.

Detail the rights and responsibilities of both the franchisor and the franchisee.

OPERATIONS MANUAL: Provide a comprehensive guide on clinic operations, including opening and closing procedures. Explain standard operating procedures for patient care, consultations, and treatments. Outline inventory management, including sourcing and storing Ayurvedic medicines and products. Describe staffing requirements and guidelines for hiring, training, and scheduling employees.

Marketing and Branding Guidelines: Define the brand identity, including logo usage, color schemes, and clinic aesthetics. Outline marketing strategies and tactics to promote the clinic locally.Provide templates for promotional materials, including brochures, posters, and digital assets.

Ayurvedic Practices and Treatments: Educate franchisees about Ayurvedic principles and practices.Detail the range of treatments and services offered in the clinic. Specify the qualifications and certifications required for Ayurvedic practitioners.

Compliance and Regulatory Requirements: Explain the legal and regulatory requirements for operating an Ayurveda clinic in the franchise's target region. Ensure compliance with health and safety standards, patient data privacy, and any necessary certifications or licensees.

Financial Reporting and Accounting: Provide a standardized financial reporting template for franchisees. Explain how to manage revenue, expenses, and financial records. Set expectations for financial audits and reporting timelines.

Support and Training: Describe the training programs and ongoing support provided by the franchisor. Offer resources for continuous education in Ayurveda and holistic health practices. Establish channels for communication and issue resolution between the franchisor and franchisees.

Site Selection and Clinic Setup: Offer guidance on selecting suitable locations for clinics. Provide specifications for clinic setup, interior design, and equipment.

Quality Assurance and Customer Service: Outline quality control measures for treatments and patient care. Define customer service standards and expectations.

Franchisee Obligations: Clearly state the responsibilities and obligations of the franchisee regarding clinic management, staffing, and adherence to brand standards. Remember to consult with legal professionals and industry experts to ensure that your documentation complies with local regulations and addresses specific requirements for an Ayurveda clinic franchise in your target market.

CHAPTER SIX

LEGAL AND FINANCIAL CONSIDERATIONS

HIGHLIGHTS

This chapter highlights the pivotal role of franchise agreements, explores financial planning essentials for Ayurveda clinics, delves into diverse funding options, and meticulously breaks down franchisee fees and costs, offering a comprehensive guide for entrepreneurs entering the holistic healthcare franchise

THE PURPOSE OF FRANCHISE AGREEMENTS AND CONTRACTS

Franchise agreements and contracts serve as the backbone of the franchising model, which has become an integral component of the global business landscape. The primary purpose of these documents is to establish a clear and legally binding understanding between the franchisor (the parent company) and the franchisee (the individual or entity operating a branch of the business). They outline the terms and conditions governing the franchisor-franchisee relationship, safeguarding both parties' interests.

KEY ELEMENTS OF FRANCHISE AGREEMENTS AND CONTRACTS

Franchise Fee and Royalties: These contracts specify the initial franchise fee, which is the cost of obtaining the franchise rights, and the ongoing royalties or fees that the franchisee must pay to the franchisor.

Territory and Location: Franchise agreements detail the geographical territory in which the franchisee is permitted to operate and often include site selection criteria for establishing the franchise location.

Operating Standards: Contracts define the standards and procedures that franchisees must adhere to, ensuring uniformity in the quality of products or services offered.

Training and Support: They outline the training and support provided by the franchisor to assist the franchisee in running the business successfully.

Intellectual Property Rights: These agreements protect the franchisor's intellectual property, including trademarks, logos, and proprietary systems, while granting the franchisee the right to use them.

Duration and Renewal: The duration of the franchise relationship and the conditions for renewal or termination are crucial aspects addressed in these documents.

Exit Strategies: The agreement may include provisions for selling the franchise or exiting the business, safeguarding the interests of both parties.

Significance of Franchise Agreements and Contracts

Legal Protection: These documents offer legal protection to both parties, reducing the risk of disputes and clarifying rights and obligations.

Consistency: They ensure consistent branding, quality, and customer experience across all franchise locations, preserving the brand's reputation.

Risk Management: By outlining operational standards and best practices, they help mitigate operational risks for franchisees.

Economic Growth: Franchising provides opportunities for aspiring entrepreneurs, contributing to economic growth by creating businesses and generating jobs.

Flexibility: These agreements can be tailored to suit the specific needs of the franchisor and franchisee, allowing for flexibility within the framework.

Conclusion: Franchise agreements and contracts are the cornerstones of the franchising business model, playing a pivotal role in shaping successful partnerships. They offer legal protection, ensure consistency, and promote economic growth while providing a structured framework for franchisors and franchisees to thrive together. As franchising continues to evolve, the significance of these documents in maintaining harmonious and profitable business relationships remains undiminished.

FINANCIAL PLANNING AND FUNDING OPTIONS FOR AYURVEDA FRANCHISE CLINIC

The healthcare industry, with its emphasis on holistic well-being and alternative medicine, has witnessed a surge in popularity. Ayurveda, a traditional Indian system of medicine, has gained global recognition for its natural and holistic approach to healthcare. Establishing an Ayurveda franchise clinic can be a lucrative and fulfilling venture, but it requires careful financial planning and the selection of appropriate funding options. This essay explores the financial aspects of setting up an Ayurveda franchise clinic and discusses various funding options available to aspiring entrepreneurs.

FINANCIAL PLANNING FOR AYURVEDA FRANCHISE CLINIC

Start-up Costs: Setting up an Ayurveda franchise clinic involves various initial expenses. These may include location rental or purchase, renovation costs, equipment procurement, licensing fees, and marketing expenses. A detailed business plan should be developed to estimate these costs accurately.

Operational Expenses: Operational expenses encompass the day-to-day costs of running the clinic. These expenses may include employee salaries, utilities, raw materials, administrative costs, and maintenance. A well-structured budget is crucial to keep track of these ongoing expenditures.

Revenue Projections: It is vital to make realistic revenue projections based on factors like patient volume, pricing strategy, and market demand. Financial forecasting helps in understanding when the clinic can break even and start generating profits. Funding Options for Ayurveda Franchise Clinic

Personal Savings: Many entrepreneurs use their personal savings as the initial source of funding. While this option provides independence and avoids debt, it also carries a certain level of risk.

Bank Loans: Traditional bank loans, including term loans and lines of credit, can be a reliable source of funding. Lenders will assess your business plan, creditworthiness, and collateral before approving the loan.

Franchisor Financing: Some Ayurveda franchise opportunities offer financing options directly from the franchisor. This can be advantageous as they understand the business model and may offer favorable terms.

Investors and Venture Capital: Seeking investments from individuals or venture capital firms can provide a significant infusion of capital. However, it often involves giving up equity or ownership stakes in the business.

Crowdfunding: Crowdfunding platforms can be used to raise capital from a large number of people who believe in your business idea. This method can be particularly useful for attracting funds from a broad base of supporters.

Government Grants and Subsidies: Various government programs offer grants and subsidies for healthcare-related businesses. Researching and applying for such opportunities can reduce the financial burden.

Alternative Lending: In recent years, alternative lending sources such as online lenders and peer-to-peer lending platforms have become popular. They often have less stringent requirements and can provide quick access to funds.

Conclusion: Starting an Ayurveda franchise clinic involves a combination of careful financial planning and selecting the right funding options. Entrepreneurs should assess their financial situation, research the costs involved, and determine which funding sources align with their business goals. A well-structured financial plan and a clear understanding of the available funding options are crucial for the success of an Ayurveda franchise clinic. It is essential to strike a balance between financing and ensuring the quality of healthcare services provided, as patient satisfaction and well-being should always be at the forefront of the business.

FRANCHISEE FEES, ROYALTIES AND OTHER COSTS FOR AYURVEDA FRANCHISE CLINIC

Setting franchisee fees, royalties, and other costs for an Ayurveda franchise clinic involves a careful balance between ensuring profitability for both the franchisor and franchisee while maintaining the attractiveness of the franchise opportunity. Here's a breakdown of these financial aspects:

Franchisee Fees:

a. Initial Franchise Fee: The initial franchise fee is a one-time payment made by the franchisee to gain access to the franchisor's brand, training, and support which dependson the brand's reputation and the level of support provided.

b. Territory Fee: In some cases, franchisors charge an additional fee for exclusive territorial rights. This ensures that no other franchise clinic from the same brand will operate within a certain radius.

Royalties:

a. Ongoing Royalty Fee: The ongoing royalty fee is typically a percentage of the franchisee's gross sales and is paid on a regular basis, often monthly. The percentage can vary depending on the level of support provided by the franchisor.

b. Marketing and Advertising Fee: Franchisees may also be required to contribute to a marketing and advertising fund. This fee could be around 2% to 4% of monthly gross sales and is used for regional or national marketing campaigns to promote the brand.

Other Costs:

a. Equipment and Inventory: Franchisees should budget for the purchase of Ayurveda equipment, herbal products, and medicinal supplies, which can vary widely depending on the size and scale of the clinic.

b. Renovation and Lease Costs: Renovating the clinic space to meet the brand's standards and lease expenses can be significant. These costs will depend on location and the condition of the premises.

c. Staffing and Training: Hiring and training qualified Ayurvedic practitioners and support staff is essential. The costs for staff salaries, benefits, and training should be included in the budget.

d. Licensing and Insurance: Franchisees must obtain the necessary licenses and insurance, which can vary by location. The cost of compliance and coverage should be considered.

e. Administrative and Technology: Budget for software, record-keeping systems, and administrative costs for the smooth operation of the clinic.

f. Working Capital: A reserve for working capital should be set aside to cover operational expenses until the clinic becomes profitable.

It's important to note that the specific fees and costs can vary greatly depending on the franchisor, the location of the clinic, and the scale of the operation. Franchisees should carefully review the franchise agreement, perform due diligence, and seek legal and financial advice to understand the full financial implications of entering into an Ayurveda franchise. Additionally, franchisors should offer transparent and comprehensive financial information to potential franchisees to ensure a successful and mutually beneficial partnership.

CHAPTER SEVEN

SETTING UP YOUR FRANCHISE CLINIC

HIGHLIGHTS

It underscores the pivotal role of location selection, the art of designing a harmonious prototype Ayurvedic clinic, and the meticulous process of sourcing medicines and equipment, offering a holistic guide for establishing a successful and authentic Ayurveda franchise clinic.

CHOOSING THE RIGHT LOCATION FOR AN AYURVEDA FRANCHISE CLINIC

The decision to open an Ayurveda franchise clinic is a significant step towards promoting holistic healthcare. However, one of the most crucial factors that can influence the success of your clinic is the choice of its location. Selecting the right location is a complex decision that involves various factors. This essay will discuss the importance of choosing the right location for an Ayurveda franchise clinic and outline the key considerations to keep in mind.

IMPORTANCE OF LOCATION

The location of an Ayurveda franchise clinic plays a pivotal role in determining its success. Here are some reasons why choosing the right location is essential:

Target Market: The location should align with your target market. It should be easily accessible to the demographic you wish to serve, such as individuals seeking alternative and holistic healthcare solutions.

Visibility: A prime location with good visibility can attract more foot traffic and potential clients. It can also enhance your clinic's brand recognition.

Fig: 7.1 Image showing different variables of marketing

Competition: Analyzing the presence of existing Ayurveda or alternative healthcare clinics in the area is crucial. A location with limited competition can be advantageous.

Infrastructure: Consider the infrastructure and amenities available in the area. Adequate parking, public transportation, and nearby facilities can make the clinic more accessible to clients.

Legal and Regulatory Considerations: Different regions may have varying regulations and licensing requirements for healthcare clinics. Ensure your chosen location complies with these regulations.

KEY CONSIDERATIONS FOR LOCATION SELECTION

Demographics: Conduct a thorough demographic analysis of the area to understand the population's age, income, health concerns, and lifestyle. This information can help tailor your clinic's services to the local community.

Competition Analysis: Identify the presence and strength of competitors in the area. If there are established Ayurveda clinics, assess their services, pricing, and reputation.

Accessibility: Choose a location that is easily accessible by both car and public transportation. The convenience of reaching your clinic will attract more clients.

Visibility: Opt for a location that offers good visibility and signage options to make your clinic stand out.

Rental Costs: Evaluate the rental or leasing costs of potential locations. Ensure that it aligns with your budget and projected revenue.

Local Regulations: Be aware of any local healthcare regulations and licensing requirements. Ensure that your clinic complies with all legal and ethical standards.

Market Research: Conduct market research to understand the demand for Ayurvedic services in the chosen area. This can help in fine-tuning your services and marketing strategies.

Conclusion: Selecting the right location for your Ayurveda franchise clinic is a critical decision that can significantly impact your clinic's success. By considering factors such as demographics, competition, accessibility, and legal requirements, you can make an informed choice that aligns with your business goals and the healthcare needs of your target market. A well-chosen location can set the foundation for a thriving Ayurveda clinic that promotes holistic well-being in the community.

DESIGNING A PROTOTYPE AYURVEDIC CLINIC

Designing a prototype Ayurvedic clinic is a complex and multifaceted endeavor that requires careful consideration of various elements, from the physical layout to the services offered.

Location and Aesthetics: Selecting the right location is crucial. An Ayurvedic clinic should ideally be situated in a serene and natural environment. The clinic's aesthetics should reflect the essence of Ayurveda, with elements such as natural materials, soothing color schemes, and calming decor.

Layout and Design: The clinic's layout should include separate areas for consultation, treatment, and relaxation. Patients' comfort and privacy should be prioritized. Incorporate natural lighting and ventilation to create a harmonious atmosphere.

Treatment Rooms: Treatment rooms should be equipped with Ayurvedic therapies in mind. This includes massage tables, steam chambers, and oil storage. Ensuring a tranquil ambiance in these spaces is essential for the therapeutic experience.

Herb Dispensary: An Ayurvedic clinic should have an herb dispensary, offering a wide range of Ayurvedic medicines and herbal products. A qualified Ayurvedic practitioner should manage this section.

Consultation and Diagnosis: Design a consultation room where practitioners can discuss patients' health concerns and perform Ayurvedic diagnostics, such as pulse reading and tongue examination.

Therapies and Services: Determine the range of Ayurvedic therapies and services to be offered, such as Abhyanga (oil massage), Panchakarma detoxification, and dietary counseling. Ensure that the clinic is well-equipped for these services.

Holistic Approach: Ayurveda emphasizes a holistic approach to health. Design the clinic to incorporate yoga and meditation spaces for overall well-being and stress reduction.

Staffing: Recruit qualified and experienced Ayurvedic practitioners, therapists, and support staff who can provide authentic and personalized care to patients.

Regulatory Compliance: Ensure that the clinic complies with local healthcare regulations and follows ethical practices, especially considering the use of herbs and traditional therapies.

Patient Education: Design an area for patient education, where individuals can learn about Ayurveda, its principles, and healthy lifestyle practices.

Technology Integration: Integrate technology for appointment scheduling, medical records, and communication with patients while keeping the clinic's essence rooted in tradition.

Sustainability: Embrace eco-friendly practices in the clinic's design and operations, using sustainable materials and energy-efficient systems.

Community Engagement: Consider community outreach and engagement programs to educate the local population about Ayurveda and its benefits.

Conclusion: Designing a prototype Ayurvedic clinic is a dynamic process that combines traditional wisdom with modern functionality. It should create a harmonious environment that promotes health and well-being in alignment with Ayurvedic principles. A well-designed Ayurvedic clinic can serve as a beacon of holistic healthcare, offering individuals an authentic and transformative experience on their path to wellness.

SOURCING MEDICINES AND EQUIPMENT FOR AN AYURVEDA CLINIC

Establishing and maintaining a well-equipped Ayurveda clinic is essential for providing effective holistic healthcare. Sourcing medicines and equipment for such a clinic requires careful planning and consideration of various factors, including the quality of products, regulatory compliance, and cost-effectiveness. This essay will explore the key aspects of sourcing medicines and equipment for an Ayurveda clinic.

Medicine Sourcing

Ayurvedic Medicine Suppliers: The first step in sourcing medicines for an Ayurveda clinic is to identify reputable Ayurvedic medicine suppliers. These suppliers should have a good track record of quality and adhere to GMP (Good Manufacturing Practices) standards.

Quality Assurance: Ensuring the quality of medicines is paramount. Ayurvedic medicines should be prepared using authentic ingredients and traditional formulations. It is crucial to conduct quality checks and verify the source of raw materials to maintain the integrity of the medicines.

Regulatory Compliance: Ayurvedic medicines must adhere to regulatory guidelines set by government authorities. Ensure that the medicines sourced comply with relevant regulations, including those related to labeling and packaging.

Traditional vs. Patented Formulations: Decide whether to stock traditional Ayurvedic formulations or patented Ayurvedic products. Traditional formulations are time-tested but may have limitations, while patented products may offer specific advantages but could be costlier.

Equipment Sourcing

Diagnostic Equipment: Ayurveda clinics may require diagnostic equipment such as pulse diagnosis devices, Nadi Pariksha instruments, and basic diagnostic tools to assess patients' health.

Treatment Equipment: Traditional Ayurvedic treatments like Panchakarma require specialized equipment like massage tables, steam chambers, and oil heaters. Ensure that these are of good quality and easy to maintain.

Herbal Preparations: Ayurvedic clinics often prepare medicines and oils in-house. Invest in equipment for grinding herbs, extracting oils, and preparing formulations.

Safety and Hygiene: Ensure that the clinic complies with hygiene and safety standards. Equip the clinic with sterilization devices for sanitation and storage solutions for herbs and medicines.

Cost Considerations: Balancing quality with cost-effectiveness is crucial. Price comparison, negotiating with suppliers, and considering long-term operational expenses are essential to make informed decisions.

Conclusion: Sourcing medicines and equipment for an Ayurveda clinic is a critical aspect of ensuring the clinic's success. It requires a delicate balance between maintaining the authenticity of Ayurvedic treatments, complying with regulations, and managing costs. By following these principles and guidelines, Ayurveda clinics can offer holistic healthcare services that meet both traditional and modern standards.

Section 3

GROWING YOUR AYURVEDA CLINIC FRANCHISE

CHAPTER EIGHT

MARKETING AND BRANDING

HIGHLIGHTS

Building an Ayurveda brand entails a profound grasp of principles, quality sourcing, innovation, and a community-centric approach. The guide explores holistic strategies, emphasizing authenticity, education, and partnerships for successful Ayurveda franchising, blending online and offline promotion to create a trusted wellness presence.

BUILD AN AYURVEDA BRAND

Building an Ayurveda brand requires a strategic approach that incorporates a deep understanding of Ayurvedic principles, effective marketing, and a commitment to quality.

As interest in holistic healing methods continues to grow, the establishment of a successful Ayurveda brand becomes increasingly relevant. The key steps to build an Ayurveda brand that is rooted in are tradition, quality, and authenticity.

Understanding Ayurvedic Principles: The foundation of an Ayurveda brand lies in a profound comprehension of Ayurvedic principles. This includes the understanding of Doshas (Vata, Pitta, Kapha), the importance of balance, and the role of diet, lifestyle, and herbal remedies. It is crucial to have Ayurvedic experts on board to ensure that the brand's products and services align with these principles.

Quality and Authenticity: Ayurveda emphasizes the use of natural ingredients and traditional formulations. To build a reputable brand, it's imperative to source high-quality, organic herbs and ingredients. Authenticity should be at the forefront, with transparency about ingredient sourcing and production processes. Third-party certifications for quality and purity can add credibility.

Research and Innovation: While preserving tradition is essential, innovation can set your brand apart. Invest in Ayurvedic research to develop new formulations or delivery methods that are more accessible and convenient for modern consumers. Combine ancient wisdom with contemporary solutions.

Product Range: Diversify your product range to cater to a broader audience. Offer herbal supplements, skincare products, wellness consultations, and even Ayurvedic education. A comprehensive approach can attract a larger customer base.

Marketing and Education: Effective marketing is vital to make your Ayurveda brand known. Use social media, content marketing, and partnerships with influencers who share an interest in holistic health. Educate your audience about Ayurveda's benefits and principles to build trust and credibility.

Sustainability: Sustainability is a growing concern for consumers. Show your commitment to the environment by using eco-friendly packaging, sustainable sourcing, and responsible manufacturing processes. This can resonate with conscious consumers and enhance your brand image.

Customer Experience: Provide excellent customer service and support. Ayurveda is a personalized system, and customers may seek guidance. Offer consultations with Ayurvedic practitioners and respond to customer queries promptly. Positive experiences can lead to repeat business and word-of-mouth recommendations.

Compliance and Certification: Ensure that your brand complies with regulatory requirements in the regions where you operate. Seek certifications or licenses if necessary to gain consumer trust and credibility.

Building Partnerships: Collaborate with Ayurvedic schools, wellness centers, and yoga studios to expand your reach. These partnerships can help you access a dedicated audience interested in holistic health.

Feedback and Improvement: Collect feedback from customers and continuously work on improving your products and services. Adapt to changing consumer needs and market trends.

Conclusion: Building an Ayurveda brand is not just a business endeavor; it's a commitment to holistic health and well-being. By staying true to Ayurvedic principles, ensuring quality and authenticity, and employing effective marketing strategies, you can create a brand that resonates with individuals seeking a balanced and healthy lifestyle. In this journey, your Ayurveda brand becomes not only a business but a trusted partner in the pursuit of well-being.

MARKETING STRATEGIES FOR AYURVEDA FRANCHISING

Ayurveda franchising offers a way to capitalize on this growing interest in traditional healing practices. Following are effective marketing strategies for Ayurveda franchising, emphasizing the need for authenticity, education, and community engagement.

Branding and Consistency: Establish a strong and consistent brand identity for your Ayurveda franchise. The brand should reflect the core principles of Ayurveda, emphasizing wellness, balance, and authenticity. Ensure that all franchise outlets maintain uniform branding to create a recognizable presence.

Educational Workshops and Seminars: Education is key in the Ayurveda industry. Organize workshops, seminars, and webinars to educate both franchisees and customers about the benefits of Ayurveda. These events can serve as valuable marketing tools, building trust and authority in the field.

Localized Marketing: Tailor marketing strategies to the specific demographics and cultural nuances of the franchise's location. Understanding the unique needs and preferences of the local community is essential for successful Ayurveda franchising.

Content Marketing: Develop a content marketing strategy to share Ayurvedic knowledge and insights. Create informative blog posts, videos, and infographics that offer valuable information about Ayurveda. Sharing this content on your website and social media channels can attract potential customers seeking wellness solutions.

Online Presence: Maintain a strong online presence by creating a user-friendly website. Incorporate search engine optimization (SEO) techniques to improve your franchise's visibility in online search results. Encourage online bookings and consultations for convenience.

Social Media Engagement: Leverage social media platforms to connect with a wider audience. Share Ayurvedic tips, success stories, and engage with followers. Social media can also serve as a platform for customer reviews and recommendations.

Loyalty Programs: Implement loyalty programs to reward frequent customers. This not only encourages repeat business but also fosters a sense of community among Ayurveda enthusiasts.

Community Involvement: Participate in local wellness events, health fairs, and community gatherings. Engaging with the community helps to build trust and create a loyal customer base. Offering free consultations or samples at these events can attract new customers.

Online Advertising: Invest in online advertising, such as pay-per-click (PPC) campaigns, on search engines and social media platforms. This can help boost visibility and reach a broader audience.

Partnerships and Collaborations: Forge partnerships with yoga studios, fitness centers, and organic food stores that align with Ayurveda's principles. Collaborations can lead to cross-promotion and introduce your franchise to a wider network of potential customers.

Customer Testimonials: Collect and showcase customer testimonials and success stories. Personal experiences are powerful marketing tools, demonstrating the effectiveness of Ayurveda treatments and products.

Franchisee Support: Provide comprehensive support and training to franchisees in terms of marketing strategies, ensuring that they can effectively promote Ayurveda within their local communities.

Conclusion: Marketing strategies for Ayurveda franchising should be a blend of tradition and innovation, reflecting the ancient wisdom of Ayurveda while adapting to the needs of the modern world. By prioritizing authenticity, education, and community engagement, Ayurveda franchises can successfully tap into the growing demand for holistic wellness solutions. In doing so, they not only become profitable businesses but also valuable contributors to the well-being of their communities.

ONLINE AND OFFLINE PROMOTION STRATEGIES FOR AYURVEDA FRANCHISING

An effective promotion strategy, combining both online and offline methods, is essential to succeed in the competitive world of wellness. This essay explores the significance of a balanced approach to online and offline promotion for Ayurveda franchising, highlighting the benefits and strategies for each.

ONLINE PROMOTION FOR AYURVEDA FRANCHISING:

Website and SEO: An informative and user-friendly website is the cornerstone of online promotion. Implementing search engine optimization (SEO) techniques ensures that the website ranks well in search results, making it easier for potential customers to find your franchise.

Social Media Marketing: Leverage popular social media platforms to engage with a broader audience. Create and share Ayurvedic content, including wellness tips, testimonials, and educational videos. Social media allows for direct interaction with followers and the promotion of franchise events and services.

Email Marketing: Email marketing remains a powerful tool for keeping customers informed about Ayurvedic treatments, offers, and events. Personalized email campaigns can nurture leads and maintain a direct line of communication with customers.

Online Advertising: Utilize digital advertising channels, such as Google Ads and social media ads, to target specific demographics and reach potential clients actively searching for holistic wellness solutions. Online ads can be highly targeted and cost-effective.

Content Marketing: Create informative and engaging content through blogs, videos, and infographics. This content can position your franchise as a trusted source of Ayurvedic knowledge, attracting organic traffic and building brand authority.

OFFLINE PROMOTION FOR AYURVEDA FRANCHISING

Wellness Workshops and Seminars: Host Ayurveda wellness workshops and seminars in your franchise locations. These events offer in-person education and engagement with the community, building trust and credibility.

Local Events and Fairs: Participate in local wellness events, health fairs, and holistic markets. These events provide an opportunity for face-to-face interaction, offering free Ayurvedic consultations and product samples.

Print Collateral: Design and distribute brochures, flyers, and informative print materials that reflect Ayurveda's principles. These materials can be placed in local businesses, clinics, and community centers.

Local Media and Public Relations: Build relationships with local media outlets and wellness influencers. Positive coverage in local newspapers, magazines, and TV segments can enhance your franchise's reputation and reach a broader local audience.

Partnerships: Collaborate with local yoga studios, fitness centers, and organic food stores that share Ayurveda's values. Cross-promotion and referral programs can expand your reach and customer base.

BALANCING ONLINE AND OFFLINE PROMOTION

Audience Segmentation: Identify your target audience and their preferences. Allocate resources based on where your audience is most active and receptive. Younger audiences may engage more with online methods, while older demographics may prefer in-person interactions.

Consistent Branding: Maintain a consistent brand identity and message across both online and offline channels. This consistency reinforces your franchise's identity and values, leading to increased recognition and trust.

Data Integration: Leverage data analytics to track the performance of online and offline campaigns. Integrating data can reveal insights into what strategies work best and inform future decisions.

Cross-Promotion: Integrate both online and offline promotion channels. For instance, direct offline events to online resources, or use QR codes on printed materials to direct customers to your website.

Conclusion: Effective promotion is fundamental to the success of Ayurveda franchising, offering a holistic approach to wellness. By blending the strengths of online promotion, with its reach and data-driven capabilities, and offline promotion, with its personal and trust-building qualities, Ayurveda franchises can effectively reach and engage with their diverse audience. This balanced approach ensures that the wisdom of Ayurveda is not only accessible but also trusted in the communities they serve, making Ayurveda franchising a successful and impactful endeavor in the world of wellness.

CHAPTER NINE

MANAGING OPERATIONS

HIGHLIGHTS

Developing a comprehensive franchise operation manual and adhering to standard operating procedures are crucial for the success of Ayurveda franchise clinics, covering aspects from staff appointments and training to efficient patient scheduling, inventory management, and meticulous patient record-keeping.

-Franchise Operation Manual
-Standard Operating Procedures
-Apponting Doctor and Staff
- Training of Staff
- Opening & Closing of Clinic
-Patients Scheduling
-Inventory Management
-Managing Patient Records

DEVELOPING A COMPREHENSIVE FRANCHISE OPERATION MANUAL

To ensure the success and uniformity of these franchises, a comprehensive Franchise Operation Manual is essential. This essay outlines the key components of such a manual, focusing on the unique aspects of an Ayurveda Franchise Clinic.

I. Executive Summary

he Executive Summary should provide an overview of the Ayurveda Franchise Clinic and its mission. It should also briefly describe the franchise operation structure, highlighting the roles and responsibilities of the franchisor and franchisee.

II. Introduction to Ayurveda

This section should educate franchisees about the principles and foundations of Ayurveda, its historical significance, and its role in modern healthcare.

III. Franchise Business Model

Explain the franchise business model, including the licensing agreement, financial terms, and the relationship between the franchisor and franchisee.

IV. Clinic Setup

Detailed guidelines on setting up the Ayurveda clinic, including location selection, interior design, and equipment requirements.

V. Staffing and Training

Provide an outline of the staff requirements, from Ayurvedic practitioners to administrative personnel. Include details on recruitment, training, and performance evaluation.

VI. Ayurvedic Treatments and Services

Explain the range of Ayurvedic treatments and services offered at the clinic. Provide information about treatment protocols, safety measures, and standards of practice.

VII. Product Inventory

Discuss the selection and management of Ayurvedic products and medicines. Include details on sourcing, storage, and inventory management.

VIII. Marketing and Branding

Outline the marketing strategies and branding guidelines for the clinic. Discuss digital marketing, traditional advertising, and community engagement.

IX. Customer Care and Relations

Provide guidelines on how to build strong customer relations, handle complaints, and maintain a high level of patient satisfaction.

X. Quality Control and Compliance

Explain the importance of quality control in Ayurveda and how to ensure compliance with relevant regulations and standards.

XI. Financial Management

Detail financial reporting and record-keeping requirements, budgeting, and revenue-sharing arrangements.

XII. Health and Safety

Discuss safety protocols, hygiene standards, and emergency response procedures within the clinic.

XIII. Maintenance and Upkeep

Provide guidelines for the routine maintenance of the clinic, equipment, and facilities.

XIV. Troubleshooting and Problem-Solving

Include a section on common challenges that may arise and solutions to address them.

XV. Appendices

This section should contain any relevant templates, forms, and additional resources for franchisees to reference.

Conclusion: Developing a Franchise Operation Manual for an Ayurveda Franchise Clinic is essential to ensure the standardized operation and growth of such ventures. This manual should serve as a comprehensive guide for franchisees, helping them understand the intricacies of running an Ayurveda clinic while upholding the brand's values and quality standards. The success of the franchise network ultimately depends on the quality of this manual and its consistent implementation across all clinics.

The Significance of Standard Operating Procedures (SOPs) in Ayurveda Franchise Clinics

To ensure consistency, quality, and the successful operation of these franchises, Standard Operating Procedures (SOPs) play a pivotal role.

I. Definition of SOPs

SOPs are detailed, step-by-step guidelines that document the standard procedures and protocols for various aspects of a business or organization. In the context of Ayurveda franchise clinics, SOPs ensure that every clinic within the franchise network follows uniform practices and maintains the integrity of the Ayurvedic system.

II. Ensuring Quality of Ayurvedic Services

SOPs are fundamental in preserving the quality of Ayurvedic services offered in franchise clinics. They define the specific processes and techniques for Ayurvedic treatments and therapies. This includes the preparation of herbal medicines, administration of therapies, and the ethical conduct of practitioners.

III. Consistency in Patient Care

SOPs promote consistency in patient care. Regardless of which franchise clinic a patient visits, they can expect a consistent level of care and treatment. This consistency is essential for building trust and ensuring patient satisfaction.

IV. Compliance with Ayurvedic Principles

SOPs guide franchise clinics in adhering to the core principles and ethics of Ayurveda. They help ensure that practitioners respect traditional knowledge, focus on the individual needs of patients, and maintain the highest standards of patient safety and well-being.

V. Training and Onboarding

SOPs serve as valuable training tools for franchise clinic staff. New employees can quickly learn the proper protocols and procedures, reducing the risk of errors and misunderstandings.

VI. Operational Efficiency

Efficiency is essential for the success of any business. SOPs streamline clinic operations, making them more efficient and cost-effective. This includes guidelines for appointment scheduling, inventory management, and record-keeping.

VII. Crisis Management and Contingency Planning

SOPs provide a structured approach to crisis management. They outline how to respond to emergencies, handle patient complaints, and manage unexpected situations with professionalism and care.

VIII. Health and Safety

Ayurveda franchise clinics are healthcare facilities, and SOPs are vital for ensuring the health and safety of both patients and staff. They detail hygiene standards, sanitation practices, and safety protocols.

IX. Adaptation and Evolution

SOPs are not static documents. They can be updated and improved over time to adapt to changing regulations, emerging best practices, and advances in Ayurvedic knowledge.

X. Brand Integrity

Consistent adherence to SOPs across franchise clinics upholds the integrity of the brand. Patients come to trust the brand as a symbol of quality and traditional healing.

Conclusion: Standard Operating Procedures are the backbone of Ayurveda franchise clinics, ensuring the consistent delivery of high-quality Ayurvedic healthcare. They not only guide operations but also serve as a testament to the franchise's commitment to preserving the essence of Ayurveda. The success of Ayurveda franchise clinics ultimately depends on the development, implementation, and continuous improvement of SOPs, making them an indispensable component of this healthcare venture.

APPOINTMENT OF AYURVEDA DOCTOR AND STAFF

Appointing the right Ayurveda doctor and staff for a franchise clinic is crucial to ensure the clinic's success and the quality of healthcare services provided. Here's a step-by-step guide on how to go about this process:

Job Descriptions and Requirements: Start by creating detailed job descriptions for the Ayurveda doctor and staff positions you need to fill.

Specify the qualifications, experience, and skills required for each role.

Highlight any certifications or licenses needed, particularly for the Ayurveda doctor.

Recruitment: Advertise the job openings through various channels, including online job boards, your clinic's website, and professional Ayurveda associations. Review resumes and applications, shortlisting candidates who meet the criteria.

Interviews: Conduct interviews to assess candidates' qualifications, experience, and cultural fit with your franchise clinic.

For the Ayurveda doctor, consider a panel interview with senior clinic staff or medical professionals to assess their clinical knowledge and approach to Ayurveda.

Reference Checks: Contact the candidates' references to verify their qualifications and work history.

Offer Letters and Contracts: Once you've selected the candidates, issue formal offer letters that outline their roles, responsibilities, compensation, and any benefits. Ensure that employment contracts are signed by both parties, clearly specifying the terms of employment.

TRAINING OF STAFF

Training the staff for a franchise Ayurveda clinic is vital to ensure that they provide high-quality care and adhere to the clinic's standards. Here's a comprehensive guide on how to effectively train your staff.

Develop a Training Plan: Create a detailed training plan that outlines the objectives, content, and timeline for staff training. Identify the key areas of training, such as Ayurvedic principles, customer service, clinic procedures, and safety protocols.

Training Materials and Resources: Prepare training materials, which may include handbooks, manuals, videos, and presentations. Gather relevant resources, textbooks, and online courses for staff reference.

Ayurvedic Principles and Practices: Provide comprehensive training on Ayurvedic principles, including the doshas, Panchakarma therapies, and herbal medicine. Include practical training sessions where staff can observe and participate in Ayurvedic treatments and consultations.

Clinic Procedures: Train staff on the specific clinic procedures, including appointment scheduling, patient intake, and record-keeping. Explain the standard operating procedures (SOPs) for the clinic and ensure staff understand and follow them.

Customer Service: Emphasize the importance of excellent customer service in healthcare. Train staff on how to interact with patients professionally, handle inquiries, and maintain a friendly and welcoming environment.

Health and Safety: Ensure that staff are well-versed in health and safety protocols, including hygiene, sanitation, and safety measures during treatments. Conduct training on emergency response procedures and first aid.

Communication Skills: Enhance staff communication skills, especially for patient consultations and relaying Ayurvedic advice. Provide guidance on effective listening and empathetic communication.

Patient Confidentiality: Emphasize the importance of patient confidentiality and train staff on the legal and ethical aspects of patient data protection.

Equipment and Technology: Familiarize staff with the equipment and technology used in the clinic, such as diagnostic tools and patient management software.

Ethical Practices: Educate staff on the ethical standards of Ayurveda, including respecting patient autonomy, informed consent, and maintaining professional boundaries.

Continuous Learning: Encourage staff to engage in continuous learning by attending workshops, seminars, and Ayurveda conferences.

Support staff in pursuing advanced certifications in Ayurveda.

Feedback and Evaluation: Implement a system for feedback and evaluation to assess staff's progress and understanding. Conduct regular assessments and provide constructive feedback to help staff improve their skills.

Team Building: Foster a sense of unity and teamwork among staff members to create a positive work environment. Organize team-building activities and workshops.

Adherence to Local Regulations: Ensure that staff are aware of and comply with local healthcare regulations and licensing requirements.

Documentation and Certification: Maintain records of staff training and certifications for future reference and regulatory compliance.

Support and Mentorship: Assign experienced staff members or mentors to guide and support new hires as they adapt to their roles.

Refresher Courses: Conduct periodic refresher courses to keep staff up-to-date with evolving Ayurvedic practices and clinic procedures.

Effective training is an ongoing process, and it is essential for staff to continuously improve their skills and knowledge in the field of Ayurveda. By investing in comprehensive training, your franchise Ayurveda clinic can provide high-quality care and maintain a strong reputation for excellence in healthcare.

OPENING AND CLOSING OF CLINIC

The opening and closing procedures for an Ayurveda clinic are critical to ensure smooth clinic operations, patient safety, and security. Here are the steps for opening and closing a clinic:

Opening Procedures:
Preparation and Setup:

Arrive at the clinic early to prepare it for the day's operations.

Check that all treatment rooms and waiting areas are clean and properly set up. Ensure that all necessary supplies and equipment are in place.

Check-In Process: Open the reception desk, computer systems, and phone lines. Prepare the check-in area for receiving patients, including having the appointment schedule ready.

Safety Checks: Verify that all safety and emergency equipment, such as fire extinguishers and first-aid kits, are in their designated locations and are functional.

Patient Record Review: Review the appointments for the day and ensure that patient records are accessible and up to date.

Staff Briefing: Hold a brief staff meeting to discuss the schedule, any specific patient needs, and clinic goals for the day.

Patient Check-In: Greet and check in patients as they arrive, making sure their appointments are confirmed.

Treatment Room Preparation: Ensure that treatment rooms are equipped with the necessary supplies, oils, herbs, and equipment for the scheduled treatments.

Closing Procedures:

Patient Check-Out: Gradually wind down patient appointments as per the clinic schedule. Provide patients with any necessary post-treatment instructions, prescriptions, or follow-up appointments.

Record Maintenance: Document all relevant patient information, treatment notes, and charges in the patient records or Electronic Health Record (EHR) system.

Inventory Check: Review and update the inventory to ensure that you have an adequate supply of products and medicines for the next day.

Clean and Sanitize: Clean and sanitize treatment rooms and any equipment used during the day. Maintain high hygiene standards.

Safety and Security: Ensure that all safety measures are in place, such as turning off equipment, locking doors and windows, and activating security systems.

Cash Handling: Count and reconcile any cash or payments received during the day. Secure the day's earnings in a safe or cash management system.

Staff Meeting: Hold a brief staff meeting to review the day's operations, discuss any issues, and plan for the next day.

Shutdown Systems: Turn off all electronic systems, including computers, phones, and lights.Secure all patient records and sensitive data.

Exit Procedures: Lock all doors and windows, ensuring that the clinic is secure. Activate any alarm or security systems in place.

Review Schedule: Review the schedule for the following day to prepare for patient appointments and staff assignments.

Effective opening and closing procedures help maintain a well-organized and secure Ayurveda clinic. They ensure that patients receive the best care and that the clinic operates efficiently while complying with safety and security standards.

PATIENTS SCHEDULING FOR AYURVEDA CLINIC

Efficient patient scheduling is crucial for the smooth operation of an Ayurveda clinic. Here are steps to help you manage patient scheduling effectively:

Appointment System: Implement an appointment scheduling system. This can be done through software, online booking platforms, or a dedicated receptionist.

Appointment Types:

Define different appointment types, such as initial consultations, follow-up visits, specific treatments, or wellness check-ups.

Staff Training: Train your clinic staff on the appointment scheduling process, emphasizing the importance of professionalism, patience, and empathy when dealing with patients.

Appointment Duration: Determine the appropriate duration for different types of appointments to ensure enough time for consultations and treatments.

Buffer Times: Allow buffer times between appointments to account for overruns, emergencies, and to give practitioners time to prepare.

Online Booking: If applicable, provide an online booking option for patients to schedule appointments at their convenience.

Patient Information: Collect essential patient information during the scheduling process, such as name, contact details, health concerns, and any relevant medical history.

Appointment Confirmation: Send appointment confirmations to patients via email, SMS, or phone call to reduce no-shows.

Reminders: Implement reminder systems to notify patients of upcoming appointments, reducing the likelihood of missed appointments.

Emergency Slots: Set aside emergency slots for patients with urgent health concerns or issues that need immediate attention.

Cancellation Policy: Establish a clear cancellation policy to manage missed appointments, including any applicable fees.

Patient Preferences: Record and consider patient preferences for specific practitioners, days, or times to enhance their experience.

Waiting Area:

Design a comfortable waiting area to ensure patients have a pleasant experience while waiting for their appointments.

Electronic Health Records (EHR): Use EHR systems to maintain patient records, making it easier to track and schedule follow-up appointments.

Optimize Staff Schedules: Schedule practitioners and staff based on their availability and expertise, ensuring patients are seen by the most suitable professional.

Peak and Off-Peak Hours: Analyze your clinic's data to identify peak and off-peak hours, helping you allocate appointments efficiently.

Regularly Review Scheduling Process: Periodically review the scheduling process to identify areas for improvement, adapt to changing patient needs, and ensure optimal clinic operation.

Patient Feedback: Encourage patients to provide feedback on their scheduling experience and the overall clinic visit, and use this information to refine your processes

Sufficient scheduling not only enhances the patient experience but also maximizes the productivity of your Ayurveda clinic. By implementing a well-organized and patient-centric appointment scheduling system, you can provide high-quality care and streamline the clinic's operations.

INVENTORY MANAGEMENT FOR FRANCHISE AYURVEDA CLINIC

Effective inventory management is crucial for the smooth operation of a franchise Ayurveda clinic. Properly managing Ayurvedic products and medicines ensures that you have the necessary supplies for patient treatments and maintains the quality of your services. Here's a guide on how to manage inventory efficiently:

Inventory Assessment: Start by conducting an initial inventory assessment to determine what products and medicines you have on hand.

Categorization: Categorize your inventory into different groups, such as herbal medicines, oils, herbs, and therapeutic products.

Inventory System: Implement an inventory management system, which can be manual or digital, to keep track of stock levels, expiration dates, and reorder points.

Reordering Process: Set up a systematic reordering process to ensure you restock items before they run out. Define reorder points for each category.

First-In, First-Out (FIFO): Adhere to the FIFO principle, meaning that the products with the earliest expiration dates should be used first to prevent wastage.

Inventory Records: Maintain detailed and accurate records of all inventory transactions, including purchases, usage, and adjustments.

Digital Inventory Software: Consider using inventory management software to streamline tracking and generate reports on stock levels, trends, and product usage.

Storage Conditions: Ensure that your inventory is stored under proper conditions, such as temperature and humidity control, to maintain product quality.

Inventory Audit: Conduct regular inventory audits to reconcile physical stock with the recorded inventory. This helps identify discrepancies and potential issues.

Expiration Tracking: Regularly check the expiration dates of Ayurvedic products and remove any expired items from the inventory.

Emergency Supplies: Maintain an emergency supply of critical items to handle unexpected increases in demand or temporary disruptions in the supply chain.

Staff Training: Train clinic staff on proper inventory management practices, emphasizing the importance of accuracy and responsible product handling.

Waste Reduction: Minimize waste by accurately estimating product demand, using FIFO, and purchasing products with a reasonable shelf life.

Security Measures: Implement security measures to prevent theft or unauthorized access to the inventory.

Documentation and Compliance: Ensure that all inventory management processes are compliant with relevant regulations, including record-keeping and product sourcing.

Regular Reporting: Generate and review regular inventory reports to identify trends, slow-moving items, and opportunities for cost savings.

Continual Improvement: Continually assess and refine your inventory management processes based on the clinic's needs and changes in the Ayurvedic product market.

Effective inventory management in an Ayurveda clinic ensures that you can provide consistent, high-quality treatments to your patients and reduces the risk of product shortages or wastage. It is an integral part of maintaining the clinic's reputation and financial stability.

MANAGING PATIENT RECORDS FOR FRANCHISE AYURVEDA CLINIC

Managing patient records in a franchise Ayurveda clinic is essential for providing quality healthcare and ensuring compliance with regulations. Here are steps to effectively manage patient records:

Establish a Record-Keeping System: Implement an organized and secure system for storing patient records, which can be either physical or digital. Digital systems are often more efficient and secure.

Patient Consent and Data Privacy: Ensure that patients provide informed consent for the collection and storage of their medical information, in compliance with data privacy regulations.

Data Entry and Maintenance: Appoint a dedicated staff member to enter and update patient data in the records system.

Maintain the records with accurate and up-to-date information.

Record Components: Patient records should include personal information, medical history, treatment notes, test results, and any other relevant health data.

Standardized Record Formats: Use standardized formats for consistency in record-keeping, making it easier for healthcare providers to access and understand patient information.

Digital Health Records (EHR): Consider implementing an Electronic Health Record (EHR) system to streamline record management, accessibility, and security.

Security Measures: Ensure that patient records, whether physical or digital, are secure and only accessible by authorized personnel. Implement encryption and access controls for digital records.

Patient Identification: Use a reliable and unique identifier for each patient, such as a medical record number, to avoid confusion and maintain privacy.

Data Backups: Regularly back up digital records to prevent data loss due to technical issues or security breaches.

Record Retention and Disposal: Establish a policy for how long patient records should be retained. Dispose of records that are no longer needed, ensuring secure and confidential destruction.

Access Logs: Maintain access logs to track who accesses patient records and when. This helps monitor compliance and security.

Consistency in Documentation: Encourage healthcare providers to maintain consistency in documenting patient information, making it easier to track changes and trends.

Staff Training: Train clinic staff on the importance of accurate record-keeping, data privacy, and compliance with healthcare regulations.

Regular Audits: Conduct regular audits of patient records to identify any discrepancies or errors.

Patient Access: Allow patients to access their own records upon request, ensuring transparency and compliance with patient rights.

CHAPTER TEN

QUALITY ASSURANCE

HIGHLIGHTS

Quality assurance in franchised Ayurveda clinics ensures consistent standards, while patient feedback becomes a linchpin in healthcare quality improvement, fostering accountability, continuous improvement, and enhanced patient-centered care.

MAINTAING QUALITY STANDARDS IN FRANCHISING AYURVEDA CLINIC

Quality assurance in a franchised Ayurveda clinic is the systematic process of ensuring that the standards of care, treatment, and overall patient experience are consistent, reliable, and in alignment with the principles of Ayurveda. This is crucial because Ayurveda, as a holistic and individualized system, requires a deep understanding of its philosophy and practices. Quality assurance in this context helps to preserve the integrity of the Ayurvedic treatment and ensures that patients receive genuine and effective care.

KEY COMPONENTS OF QUALITY ASSURANCE IN FRANCHISING AYURVEDA CLINICS INCLUDE: Standardized Protocols: Developing and implementing standardized Ayurvedic treatment protocols, ensuring that every franchisee follows the same procedures and practices, thereby maintaining consistency.

Training and Certification: Offering comprehensive training programs for Ayurvedic practitioners and ensuring that they are certified in Ayurveda, guaranteeing a certain level of expertise.

Quality Control: Regularly monitoring and auditing clinic operations, treatment procedures, and herbal preparations to maintain quality standards.

Patient Feedback: Collecting and analyzing patient feedback to make continuous improvements in service quality and patient satisfaction.

Compliance with Regulations: Ensuring that all franchise clinics adhere to local and national regulations in healthcare and Ayurveda.

Knowledge Sharing: Facilitating knowledge sharing among franchisees and encouraging them to stay updated with the latest developments in Ayurveda.

THE BENEFITS OF QUALITY ASSURANCE IN FRANCHISING AYURVEDA CLINICS ARE EXTENSIVE

Consistency: Patients can expect consistent treatment and care, regardless of which franchise clinic they visit. This consistency builds trust and credibility in the brand.

Patient Trust: Quality assurance measures reassure patients that they are receiving authentic Ayurvedic care, promoting trust and loyalty.

Brand Reputation: Maintaining high-quality standards enhances the brand's reputation, attracting more patients and potential franchisees.

Legal Compliance: Ensuring adherence to regulations protects the brand and franchisees from legal issues, fostering long-term sustainability.

Franchisee Success: Equipping franchisees with the knowledge, tools, and support for quality assurance ultimately leads to their success, which benefits the franchisor.

Holistic Healthcare: The ultimate goal of Ayurveda is to provide holistic healthcare, and quality assurance helps maintain this commitment to well-being.

In conclusion, quality assurance in franchising Ayurveda clinics is not only a necessity but a cornerstone of success. It safeguards the authenticity of Ayurvedic practices, maintains consistency, and upholds patient trust. It also benefits franchisees by providing them with the necessary tools for success, ensuring regulatory compliance, and enhancing the brand's reputation. Quality assurance in Ayurveda clinics is a win-win, fostering the growth and sustainability of this ancient yet evolving system of healthcare.

PATIENT FEEDBACK: A CRITICAL COMPONENT OF HEALTHCARE QUALITY IMPROVEMENT

Patient feedback is a vital element of the healthcare system, serving as a valuable source of information for evaluating and improving the quality of care. It offers insights into patient experiences, satisfaction levels, and areas of improvement, making it an essential tool for healthcare providers, institutions, and policymakers. Here we will explore the significance of patient feedback, its various forms, and how it drives quality improvement in healthcare.

Patient feedback encompasses the opinions, concerns, and suggestions provided by patients regarding their healthcare experiences. This feedback can take several forms, including written surveys, verbal communication, online reviews, and formal complaint procedures. It plays a multifaceted role in the healthcare system:

Quality Assessment: Patient feedback provides a comprehensive assessment of the quality of care. Patients can highlight areas where healthcare providers excel and areas that require improvement.

Enhanced Patient-Centered Care: It promotes patient-centered care by ensuring that healthcare providers understand the unique needs and preferences of individual patients.

Accountability: Patient feedback holds healthcare institutions and providers accountable for the care they deliver. It encourages transparency and the acknowledgment of issues.

Continuous Improvement: Constructive feedback helps healthcare organizations identify shortcomings and implement changes to enhance the quality of services.

Patient Satisfaction: Monitoring feedback allows healthcare providers to gauge patient satisfaction, a crucial metric for measuring service quality.

Provider-Patient Communication: Feedback improves communication between healthcare providers and patients, leading to better-informed decisions and a stronger patient-provider relationship. To effectively leverage patient feedback for quality improvement, healthcare organizations must follow a structured process:

Collection: Feedback is collected through surveys, interviews, comment cards, and digital platforms. It should be easily accessible to patients.

Analysis: Feedback is analyzed to identify common themes and trends, both positive and negative. This process often involves data analytics to extract meaningful insights.

Actionable Insights: The data is used to generate actionable insights. Healthcare organizations should prioritize areas that require immediate attention and devise improvement plans.

Implementation: Healthcare providers and institutions implement changes, which can range from revising protocols and enhancing staff training to improving the patient experience.

Monitoring and Evaluation: Continual monitoring and evaluation of the impact of changes on patient feedback help in fine-tuning the quality improvement process.

Patient feedback plays a pivotal role in shaping the healthcare landscape. The benefits of incorporating patient feedback into healthcare quality improvement are numerous.

Enhanced Patient Experience: By addressing patient concerns and preferences, healthcare providers create a more positive and tailored patient experience.

Improved Clinical Outcomes: Feedback can lead to improvements in treatment protocols and clinical outcomes, ultimately benefitting patient health.

Reduced Errors: Identification of recurring issues can help reduce medical errors and enhance patient safety.

Competitive Advantage: Healthcare institutions that actively use patient feedback to improve services often enjoy a competitive edge in the market.

Legal and Ethical Compliance: Meeting patient expectations and concerns aligns with legal and ethical obligations in healthcare.

In conclusion, patient feedback is a linchpin of healthcare quality improvement. It empowers patients, informs healthcare providers, and drives the evolution of healthcare services. The healthcare industry must prioritize the collection and analysis of patient feedback, recognizing it as an invaluable resource for elevating the quality of care and ensuring that patients receive the best possible healthcare experience.

CHAPTER ELEVEN

SUCCESS DYNAMICS

HIGHLIGHTS

This chapter outlines the essential qualities of successful franchisors and explores the symbiotic relationship dynamics between franchisors and franchisees, emphasizing trust, collaboration, and shared values for mutual success in the franchising business model.

QUALITIES OF A SUCCESSFUL FRANCHISOR

Successful franchisors typically possess the following qualities:
Strong Business Model: A proven and profitable business model is essential for attracting franchisees.

Brand Recognition: A well-established and respected brand helps attract customers and potential franchisees.

Effective Training and Support: Providing comprehensive training and ongoing support to franchisees is crucial for success.

Clear Communication: Effective communication and transparency with franchisees fosters trust and collaboration.

Quality Control: Maintaining consistent product or service quality across all franchise locations is vital.

Marketing and Advertising: A strong marketing strategy to promote the brand and support franchisees is essential.

Financial Stability: A franchisor should have the financial stability to support franchise growth and invest in marketing and infrastructure.

Legal Compliance: Compliance with franchise laws and regulations is crucial to avoid legal issues.

Adaptability: The ability to adapt to changing market conditions and franchisee needs is important for long-term success.

Innovation: Constantly seeking ways to improve and innovate the business can help maintain relevance and competitiveness.

Franchisee Selection: Careful selection of franchisees who align with the brand's values and goals is critical.

Scalability: A scalable business model that can grow and expand efficiently is important for franchisors.

Strong Leadership: Effective leadership and management skills are necessary to lead the franchise system.

Ethical Practices: Maintaining high ethical standards and treating franchisees fairly is essential for long-term success.

Risk Management: Identifying and mitigating potential risks is crucial for protecting the franchise system.

Successful franchisors combine these qualities to build a mutually beneficial relationship with franchisees and sustain a thriving franchise network.

FRANCHOSOR FRANCHISE RELATIONS

The relationship between franchisors and franchisees is a fundamental aspect of the franchise business model. Franchising is a business arrangement in which the franchisor grants the franchisee the right to operate a business using the franchisor's brand, products, and systems. This relationship is built on trust, mutual benefit, and a clear set of expectations. In this essay, we will explore the dynamics of the franchisor-franchisee relationship, its key components, and the factors that contribute to its success.

1. Mutual Interdependence: The franchisor-franchisee relationship is characterized by mutual interdependence. The franchisor provides the franchisee with a proven business concept, access to a well-established brand, training, and ongoing support. In return, the franchisee invests capital, time, and effort into operating the business. This interdependence is a cornerstone of the franchise model.

2. Brand and Intellectual Property: The franchisor grants the franchisee the right to use its brand, trademarks, and intellectual property. This is a vital aspect of the relationship, as it allows the franchisee to benefit from the brand's reputation and recognition. In return, the franchisee is responsible for upholding and promoting the brand's image and standards.

3. Training and Support: Franchisors provide training and ongoing support to franchisees. This support can encompass everything from initial training in business operations to marketing and advertising assistance. The goal is to ensure that franchisees can successfully operate their businesses while maintaining the brand's consistency.

4. Business Operations: Franchisors often provide detailed operational manuals and guidelines that specify how the business should be run. This includes everything from product quality and service standards to accounting and reporting procedures. It is the franchisee's responsibility to follow these guidelines and adhere to the franchisor's established systems.

5. Financial Considerations: The financial aspects of the franchisor-franchisee relationship are crucial. Franchisees typically pay initial franchise fees, ongoing royalties, and advertising fees to the franchisor. These financial obligations are agreed upon in the franchise agreement, and they are essential for the franchisor's continued support and the franchise system's growth.

6. Legal Framework: Franchise agreements are legally binding contracts that outline the rights and responsibilities of both parties. They establish the framework for the relationship, covering issues like territory exclusivity, termination conditions, and dispute resolution processes. A well-structured franchise agreement is essential for a harmonious relationship.

7. Communication and Feedback: Effective communication is key to a successful franchisor-franchisee relationship. Open lines of communication allow for the exchange of feedback, ideas, and concerns. Franchisees often play a crucial role in providing insights from the frontlines of the business, and franchisors need to be receptive to their input.

8. Quality Control and Standards: Maintaining consistent quality and operational standards is a top priority. Franchisors implement quality control measures to ensure that the franchisee's products and services meet the brand's expectations. This is crucial for preserving the brand's reputation.

9. Expansion and Growth: Franchisors aim to expand their brand by recruiting and supporting new franchisees. This growth benefits both parties, as it increases the franchisor's market presence and provides opportunities for franchisees to expand their own businesses.

10. Conflict Resolution: Disagreements and conflicts can arise in any business relationship. It is essential for both parties to have mechanisms in place for resolving disputes, whether through mediation, arbitration, or other agreed-upon processes. This helps maintain the overall health of the franchisor-franchisee relationship.

In conclusion, the relationship between franchisors and franchisees is a unique and symbiotic partnership. It relies on trust, collaboration, and a commitment to upholding the brand's values and standards. When managed effectively, this relationship can lead to mutual success, as franchisors expand their brand and franchisees achieve their entrepreneurial aspirations. A strong franchisor-franchisee relationship is at the heart of the franchising business model, and it is built on a foundation of shared goals and responsibilities.

CHAPTER TWELVE

FUTURE TRENDS

HIGHLIGHTS

The future of Ayurveda clinic franchising is characterized by a holistic approach, emphasis on preventive healthcare, personalization through technology, integrative health practices, education, sustainability, and global expansion, aligning with the growing demand for natural and holistic wellness in the 21st century.

FUTURE TRENDS IN FRANCHISING IN AYURVEDA CLINICS

The franchise business model has witnessed significant growth and diversification across various industries in recent years, and the field of healthcare is no exception. Ayurveda, an ancient system of natural healing, is gaining popularity worldwide for its holistic approach to health and wellness. As a result, franchising in the Ayurveda clinic sector is becoming a compelling business opportunity. Here we explore the future trends in franchising in Ayurveda clinics, highlighting the key factors that are shaping this emerging industry.

INCREASED DEMAND FOR HOLISTIC HEALTHCARE

In the modern world, people are becoming more health-conscious and are seeking alternative, holistic healthcare options. Ayurveda, with its focus on balancing the mind, body, and spirit, is uniquely positioned to cater to this demand. As a result, the Ayurveda clinic franchise industry is likely to experience sustained growth.

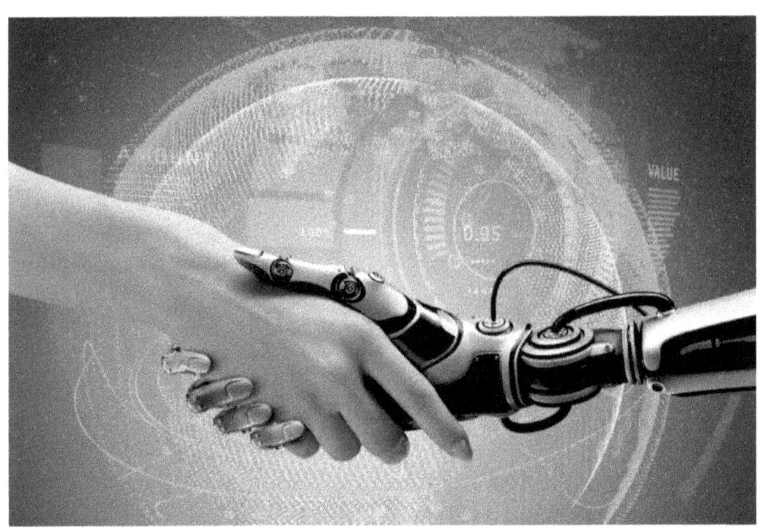

EMPHASIS ON PREVENTIVE HEALTHCARE: Preventive healthcare is gaining prominence as people look to avoid lifestyle-related diseases and improve their overall well-being. Ayurveda's preventive and wellness-focused approach aligns well with this trend, making Ayurveda clinics an attractive option for those looking to maintain their health proactively.

PERSONALIZATION AND CUSTOMIZATION: One of the strengths of Ayurveda is its personalized approach to healthcare. Ayurvedic treatments are tailored to an individual's unique constitution and health needs. Future Ayurveda clinics will likely invest in advanced technologies to enhance the customization of treatments, making them even more effective and attractive to clients.

INTEGRATIVE HEALTHCARE: The integration of Ayurveda with modern medicine is becoming a trend in healthcare. Many Ayurveda clinics are partnering with conventional medical facilities to provide patients with a more comprehensive approach to health. This integrative model is expected to gain traction in the franchising sector, allowing franchisees to tap into a broader market.

EDUCATION AND AWARENESS: As Ayurveda gains global recognition, there is a growing need for education and awareness. Future Ayurveda clinic franchises may place a strong emphasis on educating their clients about the principles and benefits of Ayurveda. This could include workshops, seminars, and wellness programs to empower individuals to take control of their health.

SUSTAINABLE AND ECO-FRIENDLY PRACTICES: Ayurveda places a strong emphasis on natural, eco-friendly practices. Future Ayurveda clinic franchises may incorporate sustainable and environmentally responsible practices into their operations, attracting clients who are environmentally conscious and health-focused.

TECHNOLOGICAL INTEGRATION: Technology is changing the way healthcare is delivered. Ayurveda clinics of the future may integrate telemedicine and digital health platforms to provide consultations and follow-ups, making Ayurveda more accessible to a wider audience.

GLOBAL EXPANSION: The Ayurveda clinic franchise model is likely to expand globally. As people around the world recognize the benefits of Ayurveda, franchises may emerge in new markets, allowing entrepreneurs to tap into this growing industry.

Case Studies Of Successful Ayurveda Clinic Franchisees

CASE STUDY: PATANJALI CHIKITSALAYA

The story of Patanjali is not like any other business in India. It is unique because it is an empire created by a baba. Yes, Baba Ramdev, the yoga guru of the masses, is the man behind the brand called PATANJALI. Baba Ramdev's name is enough to make Patanjali what it is today. He is the mascot of the brand. His years of hard work in promoting yoga and Ayurveda is what has helped him create Patanjali into a mega brand today. A not very old entrant into the FMCG sector of India, it's giving all major FMCG businesses in India a run for their money.

Along with Acharya Balkrishna, Baba Ramdev, in 2006, created a massive consumer goods company with headquarters in Haridwar, Uttrakhand. Their aim is to utilize ancient science and wisdom to produce products for customers. Its business model deals with products ranging from ayurvedic medicines, herbal products, cosmetics, and detergents to biscuits, noodles, and other snacks under one umbrella brand, Patanjali. It is a modern business empire, but there is nature and naturalness in everything they do. It resonates even in their brand slogan that states Prakriti ka Aashirwaad, i.e. blessing from nature. It has a massive network of around 4500 retail counters to sell about 900 varieties of products. It also has 10K plus Patanjali Chikitshalay (clinic) and Arogya Kendras (wellness centers) all over the country.

Patanjali Clinics (Patanjali Chikitsalayas) are being set up in different tier cities in India. The patients that come to these clinics eventually buy products from its stores and become customers of the company.

Besides, the Arogya Kendras (wellness centers) that they have also help sell its products. The yoga teachers working herein suggest fitness exercises and Patanjali's ayurvedic medicines and supplements, generating revenue for the company.

Branding and Promotion

Patanjali has been able to save huge money by not engaging any celebrities in its advertising campaigns. Baba Ramdev is the sole face of Patanjali. He is a brand himself, a yoga guru followed by millions. His cult status helps to promote the products. His image as prakritik person and believer of Ayurveda has created a perception of good health and wellness among the masses. Perhaps no other celebrity could have expanded Patanjali at a breakneck speed as Baba did.

The other benefit of putting Ayurveda and ancient wisdom to use lets Patanjali gets tax exemption as well. It has also helped Patanjali expand its manufacturing units on lands bought at discounted rates.

In the conclusion, I can only say that Patanjali's success story is an inspiration for all. This is a case for study due to its unique and successful business model that grew on a loyal customer base and word of mouth. It is the story of a baba who grew from being a yoga guru to a successful businessman.

Source: https://lakhimijc.wordpress.com/2022/10/23/growth-of-patanjali-the-mega-brand-of-india-a-case-for-study/

CASE STUDY: JIVA AYURVEDA

Background: Jiva Ayurveda is a prominent Ayurvedic healthcare and wellness company founded by Dr. Partap Chauhan in 1992. The company focuses on providing personalized Ayurvedic treatments and products for various health conditions.

KEY FACTORS FOR SUCCESS

Personalized Consultations: Jiva Ayurveda offers personalized online and in-person consultations with Ayurvedic doctors. This one-on-one approach helps tailor treatment plans to individual health needs.

Traditional Ayurvedic Treatments: The Company follows traditional Ayurvedic principles and treatments, incorporating herbal remedies and lifestyle recommendations.

Telemedicine: Jiva Ayurveda embraced telemedicine early on, allowing patients from across the world to access Ayurvedic healthcare services remotely.

Ayurvedic Education: The Company provides Ayurvedic education and training, contributing to the propagation of Ayurvedic knowledge and expertise.

Research and Development: Jiva Ayurveda invests in research and development, aiming to bridge the gap between traditional Ayurveda and modern healthcare.

Quality Control: The Company maintains high standards of quality control in its manufacturing processes, ensuring the authenticity and efficacy of its products.

Results: Jiva Ayurveda has carved a niche in the Ayurvedic healthcare and wellness sector. Its focus on personalized consultations, traditional Ayurvedic treatments, telemedicine, education, research, and quality control has established it as a reliable and respected provider of Ayurvedic healthcare services and products.

This case study illustrates how a commitment to personalized care, modern telemedicine, education, research, and quality standards can lead to the success of an Ayurveda venture. Jiva Ayurveda has contributed to the accessibility and credibility of Ayurveda in the healthcare industry by combining tradition with modern healthcare practices.

CASE STUDY: MAHARISHI AYURVEDA

Background: Maharishi Ayurveda is a globally recognized Ayurvedic company founded by Maharishi Mahesh Yogi in the 1980s. The company's mission is to promote Ayurveda's holistic approach to health and well-being.

KEY FACTORS FOR SUCCESS

Spiritual Guidance: Maharishi Mahesh Yogi's spiritual teachings and his association with transcendental meditation added a unique dimension to the brand and attracted a dedicated following.

Global Reach: Maharishi Ayurveda successfully expanded its presence worldwide, making Ayurvedic products and practices accessible to a global audience.

Ayurvedic Wellness Centers: The Company established Ayurvedic wellness centers that offer consultations, treatments, and holistic programs, providing a comprehensive Ayurvedic experience.

Purity and Authenticity: Maharishi Ayurveda places a strong emphasis on purity and authenticity in its products, sourcing herbs and ingredients from their own organic farms.

Ayurvedic Education: The Company offers Ayurvedic education, including courses and certifications, contributing to the spread of Ayurvedic knowledge.

Sustainability: Maharishi Ayurveda has also embraced sustainable and eco-friendly practices in its operations, aligning with environmentally conscious consumers.

Results: Maharishi Ayurveda has achieved global recognition for its commitment to Ayurvedic principles, its unique spiritual dimension, wellness centers, authenticity, education, and sustainability. The brand has played a significant role in bringing Ayurveda to a worldwide audience.

This case study demonstrates how a blend of spiritual guidance, global reach, holistic wellness centers, purity, education, and sustainability can lead to the success of an Ayurveda venture on an international scale. Maharishi Ayurveda's fusion of traditional Ayurveda with spiritual and global elements has been instrumental in making Ayurveda a global wellness phenomenon.

CASE STUDY: BAIDYANATH GROUP

Background: The Baidyanath Group is one of India's oldest and most respected Ayurvedic companies, with a history dating back to 1917. The company was founded by Pandit Ram Dayal Joshi and is known for its traditional Ayurvedic formulations.

KEY FACTORS FOR SUCCESS

Ayurvedic Healthcare Centers: The Company operates Ayurvedic healthcare centers and clinics, providing access to expert consultations and Ayurvedic treatments.

Heritage and Legacy: The Baidyanath Group's long-standing legacy and commitment to Ayurveda have earned it a reputation for authenticity and trustworthiness in the Ayurvedic market.

Formulation Expertise: The Company has preserved and continued to develop traditional Ayurvedic formulations, which are based on centuries-old knowledge and practices. This expertise is reflected in their product range.

Modernization and Quality Standards: While maintaining traditional practices, Baidyanath has modernized its manufacturing and quality control processes, ensuring that its products meet contemporary standards.

Research and Development: The Company invests in Ayurvedic research and product development to adapt to evolving consumer needs while remaining true to the principles of Ayurveda.

Extensive Distribution Network: Baidyanath has a well-established distribution network, allowing its products to reach a broad customer base across India and globally.

Results: The Baidyanath Group has successfully maintained its position as a leading Ayurvedic company for over a century. Its commitment to heritage, formulation expertise, quality, research, distribution, and healthcare services has contributed to its enduring success. The company continues to play a significant role in promoting Ayurveda as a holistic wellness solution.

This case study showcases how the preservation of traditional knowledge, modernization, and a commitment to quality and research can lead to the long-term success of an Ayurveda venture, even in a competitive and evolving market.

CASE STUDY: VHCA HAIR CLINIC

VHCA HAIR CLINIC: World's 1st Ayurveda Hair Clinic Chain

In the realm of personal aesthetics and self-confidence, hair plays a pivotal role. It's not just a part of our physical appearance, but a reflection of our identity and personality. Recognizing the significance of hair in people's lives, VHCA Hair Clinic has emerged as a beacon of hope and trust, offering comprehensive solutions for various hair-related concerns leveraging the AYURVEDA methodology. With a commitment to excellence, founded in 1998 by renowned Ayurveda Trichologist Dr Mukesh Aggarwal, on the principles of professionalism, innovation, and customer-centricity, VHCA Hair Clinic is backed by research based Ayurveda medicines and cutting-edge technology. From hair loss/thinning/premature greying/dandruff/baldness problems to more complex issues like alopecia areata/trichotillomania and scalp disorders, VHCA Hair Clinic offers a diverse range of treatments tailored to individual needs.

One of the cornerstones of VHCA Hair Clinic's success is its team of experienced and skilled professionals. The clinic boasts a roster of Ayurveda Trichologists & Hair Technicians who possess a deep understanding of the science behind hair health. VHCA Hair Clinic is known for its state-of-the-art procedures like PRP/GFC/HRP/Laser/ Hair Patch/Wig. Furthermore, VHCA Hair Clinic's dedication to transparency and ethical practices has earned it a loyal clientele and has a 95% patient satisfaction.

CHALLENGES

Hair Problems: Many clients suffered from various hair issues, including hair loss, dandruff, premature graying, and scalp conditions.

Competition: The clinic faced competition from conventional hair treatment centers and modern hair transplant clinics.

Awareness: Limited awareness about Ayurvedic treatments for hair care.

Solutions:

Holistic Approach: Dr. Aggarwal and his team employed a holistic approach to diagnose and treat hair problems. They focused on understanding the root causes of hair issues, including diet, lifestyle, and stress.

Customized Treatments: Tailored Ayurvedic treatments were offered to each client based on their unique hair and body constitution (Prakriti).

Herbal Products: The clinic developed its line of Ayurvedic hair care products, including oils, shampoos, and herbal supplements.

Educational Workshops: Regular workshops and seminars were conducted to raise awareness about Ayurvedic practices for hair care.

Online Presence: The clinic maintained an active online presence, offering virtual consultations and informative content on their website and social media.

Results:

Patient Satisfaction: Over the years, the clinic saw a significant increase in patient satisfaction as clients experienced visible improvements in their hair health.

Word of Mouth: Satisfied clients became advocates and referred more individuals to the clinic.

Revenue Growth: The clinic's revenue steadily increased, driven by the sale of their herbal products and services.

Strong Reputation: Dr. Aggarwal's expertise and the clinic's holistic approach contributed to a strong reputation in the community.

Future Directions:

Expansion: The clinic is expending through franchising and has a vision of 100 clinics till 2025 to serve a broader client base.

Research: Dr. Aggarwal and his dedicated research team are doing continue research in ayurvedic trichology.

Digital Outreach: Continue leveraging online platforms for educational content and consultations.

This case study highlights how an Ayurvedic hair clinic successfully addressed hair-related issues through a holistic approach, customized treatments, and a combination of traditional and modern strategies. In conclusion, VHCA Hair Clinic has become synonymous with quality, trust, and expertise in the realm of hair care and restoration.

Resources and References

PROMINENT AYURVEDIC TEXTS:

Charaka Samhita: Authored by Charaka, it is one of the foundational texts of Ayurveda, focusing on general medicine and diagnosis.

Sushruta Samhita: Attributed to Sushruta, this text primarily deals with surgery, including techniques and instruments.

Ashtanga Hridaya: Written by Vagbhata, it's a concise compilation of Ayurvedic knowledge, combining Charaka and Sushruta Samhitas.

Madhava Nidanam: Focusing on diagnostics, this text is authored by Madhavakara.

Bhaishajya Ratnavali: A comprehensive work on Ayurvedic therapeutics authored by Govind Das.

Kashyapa Samhita: Attributed to Kashyapa, it emphasizes pediatrics and gynecology.

Harita Samhita: This text covers toxicology and antidotes.

Yoga Ratnakara: An Ayurvedic text that incorporates knowledge of Ayurveda and yoga practices.

Chakradatta: An ancient text that elaborates on various diseases and their treatments.

Bhavaprakasha: A comprehensive text on Ayurvedic materia medica, authored by Bhavamishra.

Sharngadhara Samhita: Another important text on Ayurvedic pharmacology, which complements the knowledge from Charaka and Sushruta Samhitas.

Nighantu Sangraha: A classic Ayurvedic text that deals with Ayurvedic pharmacology and medicinal plants.

Rasa Ratna Samuchaya: Focuses on Ayurvedic alchemy and the use of minerals and metals in medicine.

Hatha Yoga Pradipika: While not an Ayurvedic text, it contains valuable information on yogic practices and their connection to Ayurveda.

Rasendra Sara Sangraha: An important text on Rasashastra (the science of mercury and metals) and its applications in Ayurvedic medicine.

Sahasrayogam: A compendium of Ayurvedic formulations and prescriptions.

Rasa Tarangini: A classical text on Rasashastra, which deals with the preparation of metallic and mineral medicines.

Shalihotra Samhita: A text dedicated to veterinary medicine and animal care.

Agnivesha Samhita: Often considered one of the oldest texts on Ayurvedic medicine, it's the basis for the Charaka Samhita.

BOOKS BY AYUSH DEPARTMENT

The Ayush Department, part of the Indian government, has published and recommended various books and documents related to traditional Indian systems of medicine and healthcare. Some of these include:

AYURVEDIC PHARMACOPOEIA OF INDIA
NATIONAL AYURVEDIC FORMULARY OF INDIA

Publications on traditional Indian systems of medicine research, education, and practice.

The Ayush Department periodically releases and updates these documents and publications to promote and standardize the practices and medicines of Ayurveda, Yoga, Naturopathy, Unani, Siddha, and Homeopathy in India. You can find these publications on their official website or through authorized bookstores and publications.

National Ayush Morbidity and Standardized Terminologies
Standard Treatment Guidelines for Ayurveda, Siddha, and Unani

GOVERNMENT AYURVEDA ORGANISATIONS

Here are some Indian government Ayurveda organizations:

Ministry of Ayurveda, Yoga & Naturopathy, Unani, Siddha, and Homoeopathy (AYUSH)

Address: MINISTRY OF AYUSH, AYUSH BHAWAN, B Block, GPO Complex, INA, NEW DELHI - 110023

Phone No: 011-24648354

Email: support-moayush@nic.in

Central Council for Research in Ayurvedic Sciences (CCRAS)

Jawahar Lal Nehru Bhartiya Chikitsa Avum Homeopathy Anusandhan Bhavan

No.61-65, Institutional Area, Opp. 'D' Block, Janakpuri,

New Delhi - 110058 (India)

Telephone: 91-011-28525862/28525897/28525852

National Commission for Indian System of Medicine (NCISM)
Address: 61-65, Institutional Area, Janakpuri "D" Block, New Delhi-110058
Email: secretary@ncismindia.org
Phone: + 91-11-28525464 / +91-11-28522519

National Institute of Ayurveda (NIA)
Jorawar Singh Gate, Amer Road
JAIPUR - 302002 (RAJ.) INDIA
Telephone: 91-141-2635816

All India Institute of Ayurveda (AIIA)
Mathura Road, Goutampuri
Sarita Vihar, Delhi 1100076
Ph: 011-26950401/402
Email: contact-us@aiia.gov.in

National Medicinal Plants Board (NMPB)
Ministry of AYUSH
Government of India
Indian Red Cross Society (IRCS),
Annexe Building, 1st & 2nd floor,1 Red Cross Road, New Delhi-110001,
Website : www.nmpb.nic.in
Tel : 011-23721840
E-Mail ID : info-nmpb@nic.in

State Ayurvedic Colleges and Hospitals
State Ayurveda Councils and Boards

These organizations play vital roles in promoting traditional Indian systems of medicine, research, education, and healthcare.

INDIAN AYURVEDIC ASSOCIATIONS

There are several Ayurvedic associations in India. Here are a few prominent ones:

All India Ayurvedic Congress (AIAC): AIAC is one of the oldest and most influential Ayurvedic associations in India. It promotes Ayurveda and traditional Indian medicine.

The National Integrated Medical Association (NIMA): is an Indian non-governmental organization of general practitioners educated in Ayurveda system of medicine which includes study of Modern Medicine and knowledge of ayurveda/unani/siddha with scientific approach. NIMA is officially established in 1971 with the motive to promote scientific integration of Modern Medicine & Ancient Indian Medicine i.e. ayurveda/unani/siddha.

National Ayurveda Students and Youth Association (NASYA): NASYA is a youth-oriented organization in India that focuses on promoting Ayurveda among students and young practitioners.

National Ayurvedic Medical Association (NAMA): NAMA is an organization that represents Ayurvedic professionals in India, aiming to advance the practice of Ayurveda.

Ayurveda Medical Association of India (AMAI): AMAI is an association that brings together Ayurvedic doctors and practitioners to promote Ayurvedic healthcare.

International Association for Ayurveda (IAA): While not limited to India, IAA has a presence in the country and promotes Ayurveda worldwide.

Ayurvedic Drug Manufacturers Association (ADMA): ADMA represents the interests of Ayurvedic pharmaceutical companies in India.

Ayurvedic Point of Care (APOC): APOC is a non-profit organization that focuses on Ayurvedic healthcare and research.

Association of Ayurvedic Physicians of Kerala (AAPK): AAPK is a regional association of Ayurvedic doctors in Kerala, a state known for its strong Ayurvedic tradition.

Ayurveda Pharmacy Manufacturers' Association (APMA): APMA represents the interests of Ayurvedic pharmacy manufacturers in the country.

Indian Academy of Ayurveda (IAA): IAA is dedicated to the promotion of Ayurveda through research, education, and advocacy.

Ayurvedic Graduates Medical Association (AGMA): AGMA is an association of Ayurvedic graduates who work to advance the profession and education of Ayurvedic medicine.

All India Association of Ayurvedic Graduates (AIAAG): AIAAG works to protect the rights and interests of Ayurvedic graduates and practitioners.

Indian Institute of Ayurvedic Pharmaceutical Sciences (IIAPS): IIAPS specializes in Ayurvedic pharmaceutical education and research.

Ayurveda Medical Association of India (AMAI): AMAI is another regional association representing Ayurvedic doctors and practitioners in different parts of the country.

Indian Institute of Ayurveda and Integrative Medicine (IIAIM): IIAIM is an institute that focuses on research and education in Ayurveda and integrative medicine.

Ayurveda Hospital Management Association (AHMA): AHMA is dedicated to improving the management and administration of Ayurvedic hospitals and healthcare facilities.

Ayurveda Doctors Association of India (ADAI): ADAI represents Ayurvedic doctors and practitioners across the country, advocating for the profession.

National Ayurvedic Pharmacy Association (NAPA): NAPA is an organization focused on Ayurvedic pharmacy and medication standards.

These organizations continue to play vital roles in the development and promotion of Ayurveda in India.

GLOBAL AYURVEDA ASSOCIATIONS

There are several global Ayurveda associations and organizations that promote and support the practice of Ayurveda worldwide. Some of them include:

World Ayurveda Foundation (WAF): A non-profit organization that aims to promote Ayurveda internationally and facilitate research and education in this field.

International Association of Ayurveda (IAA): A global organization that focuses on the standardization and promotion of Ayurvedic education and practice.

Ayurveda International Academy (AIA): An organization that offers Ayurveda education and certification programs to individuals and professionals worldwide.

National Ayurvedic Medical Association (NAMA): While primarily based in the United States, NAMA has members and partnerships worldwide and is dedicated to promoting Ayurveda and ensuring its integrity.

European Ayurveda Association (EUAA): Focused on promoting Ayurveda in Europe, this association connects Ayurvedic practitioners, educators, and enthusiasts across the continent.

Ayurveda Association of Canada (AAC): This organization is dedicated to promoting Ayurveda in Canada, supporting Ayurvedic practitioners, and providing resources for those interested in Ayurveda.

Ayurveda Association of Singapore (AAOS): Focused on promoting Ayurveda in Singapore and the surrounding region, AAOS works to create awareness about Ayurveda and its benefits.

Ayurveda Association of South Africa (AASA): AASA aims to connect Ayurvedic practitioners, educators, and enthusiasts in South Africa and promote the practice of Ayurveda in the country.

Ayurveda Association of New Zealand: This organization works to support Ayurvedic practitioners, educate the public about Ayurveda, and promote the practice in New Zealand.

Ayurveda Association of Australia: Dedicated to promoting Ayurveda in Australia, this association provides information, resources, and networking opportunities for Ayurvedic practitioners and enthusiasts.

Ayurveda Practitioners' Association in the UK (APA-UK): APA-UK supports Ayurvedic practitioners in the United Kingdom and promotes Ayurveda in the region.

Ayurveda Association of Malaysia: This association focuses on Ayurveda's development and recognition in Malaysia, connecting practitioners and enthusiasts.

Ayurveda Practitioners Association of North America (APNA): APNA serves Ayurvedic practitioners and supporters in North America, facilitating networking and education.

Ayurveda Association of Latin America (AALA): AALA is dedicated to promoting Ayurveda in Latin American countries and connecting practitioners in the region.

Ayurveda Association of the Czech Republic: This organization works to establish Ayurveda in the Czech Republic and offers resources and support for practitioners and enthusiasts.

Association of Ayurvedic Professionals of North America (AAPNA): AAPNA promotes Ayurveda in North America and connects professionals and students in the field.

Ayurveda Association of Ghana: This association seeks to raise awareness of Ayurveda in Ghana and promote its practice and education.

Ayurveda Association of the Netherlands: This organization is dedicated to promoting Ayurveda in the Netherlands and connecting practitioners in the country.

Ayurveda Medical Association of India (AMAI): AMAI represents Ayurvedic medical practitioners in India and advocates for the interests of Ayurvedic doctors.

Ayurveda Practitioners' Association of Sri Lanka: This association supports Ayurvedic practitioners in Sri Lanka and works to promote traditional Ayurvedic medicine in the country.

Ayurveda Association of South Korea: Focused on Ayurveda's promotion in South Korea, this association connects Ayurvedic practitioners and enthusiasts in the country.

INDEX

www.ingramcontent.com/pod-product-compliance
Lightning Source LLC
LaVergne TN
LVHW021155160826
845679LV00024B/2136

* 9 7 9 8 8 9 1 8 6 6 1 9 5 *